Children's Booklist

≥●

compiled by

The Children's Committee of
The Theosophical Society
Pasadena, California

Contents

Introduction 3
Picture Books 5
Fiction 15
Myths and Tales 31
Religions of the World 37
Poetry 41
Science and Nature: Nonfiction and Fiction 45
Nonfiction and Biography 51
Resource Books for Adults 57
Some Sources for Finding More Children's Books 61

With special thanks to the staff of the Newport Way Branch of the King County Library System, Washington, for their extensive efforts in locating many books reviewed in compiling this list; and to the staffs of the Altadena and Pasadena public libraries, California, for their able assistance.

First Edition © 1990 Theosophical University Press
Second & Expanded Edition © 2005 Theosophical University Press

Post Office Box C, Pasadena, California 91109-7107
www.theosociety.org

All rights reserved. Printed on recycled, acid-free paper.

ISBN 1-55700-176-6

Printed at Theosophical University Press, Pasadena, California

Introduction

For the child, whose sense of wonder is boundless, books that speak to the heart and stretch the imagination are vital friends. They share great experiences and emotions with children, build respect for all life, and help broaden viewpoints and values.

This list represents a cross-section of the many fine publications available in libraries and/or bookstores. It brings together a wide range of titles selected not only for their literary and artistic quality but for their universality and contribution to emotional, intellectual, and spiritual growth. Many deal constructively with social and environmental issues; others speak more to the imagination and to what it means to be a human being.

While the majority of books are for boys and girls up to 15 years of age, some are also suitable for older readers. The ages suggested refer to content and interest level, not to the child's reading level. They are only approximations to aid adults in judging which titles may meet a particular child's needs, personality, and stage of maturity. Each child is unique and relates to a story from his or her own inner self and experience — and this identity with a story is part of the magic of books.

We do not include publisher information as many children's books are published by more than one publisher and in many editions, and go in and out of print. *Books in Print* or bookstore inquiry will reveal if the title is in print at present. A library catalog or librarian can quickly determine if the title is available at a given library — the list was, in fact, compiled with the idea that parents obtain most of their children's reading material from library collections rather than bookstores.

Picture Books*

Ada, Alma Flor, *The Gold Coin* (6-10). An old woman's goodness and generosity teaches a thief to value more than gold.

Alexander, Lloyd, *The King's Fountain* (4-7). A poor man's honesty and courage persuade a king to consider his people's interests.

Aliki, *The Two of Them* (4-7). The loving relationship between a grandfather and granddaughter; after his death, her acceptance of life's continuity.

Allen, Thomas B., *Granddaddy's Farm* (6-10). Beautiful pencil drawings bring to life the author's summers in rural Tennessee.

Anderson, C. W., *The Crooked Colt* (3-7). A colt succeeds through perseverance and love. Also the *Blaze Pony* series (3-8).

Anno, Mitsumasa, *Topsy-Turvies: Pictures to Stretch the Imagination* (4-8). Escher-like perspective illusions for children.

Aragon, Jane Chelsea, *Salt Hands* (3-7). In the middle of the night a young girl watches a deer that comes and licks salt from her hands.

Ardizzone, Edward, *Little Tim and the Brave Sea Captain* (3-8). A little boy who wishes to become a sailor stows away on a steamer and has exciting adventures; first in a series.

Atwood, Ann, *The Little Circle* (4-7). A little circle's search to find itself in nature, illustrated with photographs.

Balgassi, Haemi, *Peacebound Trains* (5-9). Story of a family's separation and escape from Seoul during the Korean War; based on a true story.

Bang, Molly, *When Sophie Gets Angry — Really, Really Angry . . .* (2-8). A little girl turns to nature to get over her anger.

Barasch, Lynne, *Radio Rescue* (6-11). A boy's enthusiasm for being an amateur radio operator in the 1920s allows him to contact people around the world, and to help in emergencies; based on a true story.

---

*Further picture books appear in other subject sections, particularly under Myths and Tales, Religions of the World, and Science and Nature.

Barker, Cicely Mary, *Flower Fairy Series* (2-6). Accurate paintings of plants, shown with their "fairies," with poems giving information about the plants. Series includes "Spring," "Summer," "Trees," "Garden," and many more.

Barrett, Judi, *Cloudy with a Chance of Meatballs* (4-12). Grandpa's tall tale about the disaster that overwhelms a city where food and drink fall from the sky.

Bauer, Caroline Feller, *Midnight Snowman* (4-8). Neighborhood parents and children enjoy making a snowman together late one night.

Baylor, Byrd, *Before You Came This Way* (4-up). Rock paintings in a deserted canyon lead to a discussion of ancient peoples.

—— *The Way to Start a Day* (5-up). The many ways people of the world, past and present, greet the new day.

Bemelmans, Ludwig, *Parsley* (4-7). Friendship and helpfulness between a stag and an old, twisted tree. Also the *Madeliene* series (4-7).

Berger, Barbara, *Animalia* (5-up). Thirteen short tales from various cultures about people who have lived gently with animals.

—— *Grandfather Twilight* (3-7). Twilight personified as an old man brings the night in a fascinating bedtime story without words.

Beskow, Elsa, *Ollie's Ski Trip* (4-8). A young Swedish boy's adventures with Jack Frost and King Winter.

—— *Peter and the Blueberry Children* (4-8). Imaginative pictures bring to life Peter's adventures with the inhabitants of the Swedish countryside. Also *Around the Year* (4-7).

Blood, Charles L., and Martin Link, *The Goat in the Rug* (3-8). Charming story of a Navaho weaver told by her pet goat.

Booth, Barbara D., *Mandy* (6-11). A deaf girl living with her grandmother copes successfully with everyday tasks and a storm in the woods.

Borack, Barbara, *Grandpa* (4-9). A little girl describes her feelings about her grandfather through the experiences they share together.

Bornstein, Ruth, *Little Gorilla* (2-6). Everyone loves the little gorilla, even after he grows up.

Brett, Molly, *The Runaway Fairy* (3-6). Charmingly illustrated story of a rose fairy who leaves the garden to visit her country cousins.

Picture Books

Bright, Robert, *Georgie* (3-7). A gentle little ghost in a New England village finds that there is no place like home; first of a series.

Brown, Margaret Wise, *Goodnight Moon* (2-5). Peaceful bedtime story by the author of many children's favorites.

Browne, Anthony, *Gorilla* (5-9). A lonely girl, neglected by her busy father, is befriended by a magical gorilla.

Brunhoff, Jean de, *The Story of Babar* (3-8). This first of seven stories about a little elephant's adventures tells of his life in the city and his return to the jungle. Series continued by the author's son Laurent.

Buehner, Caralyn, *Fanny's Dream* (4-8). Sturdy farm girl hopes to marry a prince like Cinderella did, but is happier with a farmer.

Bulla, Clyde Robert, *The Christmas Coat* (4-7). Two brothers learn to cooperate when they must fix a neighbor's ruined Christmas present.

—— *The Poppy Seeds* (4-8). A boy's generosity teaches an old man to share and care; set in Mexico. Also *Daniel's Duck* (5-7), an easy-to-read book.

Bunting, Eve, *Smoky Night* (5-up). Displaced because of rioting in their neighborhood, people who resented each other are brought together.

—— *Sunshine Home* (6-11). Family members learn how much they love and need each other, and the importance of being honest about their feelings, when grandmother enters a rest home. Also *Fly Away Home* (5-12), about homelessness.

—— *The Wall* (5-8). Sensitively-told story of a boy who visits the Vietnam War Memorial in Washington DC with his father, where they find his grandfather's name.

Burningham, John, *Granpa* (4-7). Whimsical vignettes of a little girl and her grandfather enjoying each other's company.

Burton, Virginia Lee, *The Little House* (3-8). A happy country house is surrounded by the city, rescued, and moved back to the country.

Buscaglia, Leo F., *The Fall of Freddie the Leaf* (4-up). A "story of life for all ages" explores change and death, using the natural cycle of the seasons.

Caines, Jeanette, *Just Us Women* (6-9). A girl and her favorite aunt enjoy planning a car trip and then doing what they enjoy most en route.

Carle, Eric, *The Mixed-Up Chameleon* (3-7). Amusing story of a chameleon who, when his wish to be like other animals in the zoo comes true, realizes the value of being himself.

Carlstrom, Nancy White, *Grandpappy* (5-11). Carefully observed moments during a boy's summer visit with his grandfather bring out the special relationship between them.

Church, Kristine, *My Brother John* (3-7). An older brother is braver and bigger, but his little sister is more fearless about one thing.

Crystal, Billy, *I Already Know I Love You* (3-7). A first-time grandfather anticipates all the fun he'll have with his new grandchild.

Curle, Jock, *The Four Good Friends* (4-7). A grumpy man learns the value of kindness and hospitality.

Curtis, Chara M., *All I See Is Part of Me* (3-12). Brings out simply the oneness of each person with the universe, and the spiritual basis of existence.

Damjan, Mischa, *Atuk* (5-10). After slaying the wolf who killed his puppy, an Eskimo boy discovers that hate and revenge bring no satisfaction.

Davis, Maggie S., *Something Magic* (4-9). A look back at summers spent at her grandmother's house in Maine, the shared joys and sorrows, and the "magic" inside that we all share.

Demi, *The Empty Pot* (4-10). Beautiful, Chinese-style illustrations enhance the story of how a boy's honesty wins him the Emperor's throne; continued in *The Greatest Power*.

—— *Liang and the Magic Paintbrush* (4-7). With a magic paintbrush, a poor boy paints pictures which come to life.

De Paola, Tomie, *The Hunter and the Animals* (2-6). Wordless book about a hunter becoming friends with the animals.

—— *Now One Foot, Now the Other* (6-12). Touching story of the close relationship between a little boy and his grandfather, which continues as the boy helps his grandfather recover from a stroke.

De Regniers, Beatrice Schenk, *A Little House of Your Own* (3-7). Expresses charmingly each person's need for a special place.

DiSalvo-Ryan, DyAnne, *Uncle Willie and the Soup Kitchen* (5-8). A boy helps his uncle and learns that soup kitchens are busy, friendly places for helping others.

Eisenberg, Phyllis Rose, *You're My Nikki* (4-7). A little girl needs reassurance that she won't be forgotten when her mother goes back to work.

Ets, Marie Hall, *In the Forest* (2-6). A boy goes for a walk in the forest blowing his trumpet, and is joined by a parade of animals.

Picture Books

—— *Mister Penny* (4-8). Mr. Penny's lazy animals learn the satisfaction of helping and working. Also *Play with Me* (3-6).

Falconer, Ian, *Olivia* (4-11). Energetic, feisty little pig enjoys her day; whimsical illustrations.

Flack, Majorie, *Angus and the Cat* (3-6). Gentle story of a Scottie dog who chases the new cat in his house for several days, and then finds they've become friends; first of a series. Also *The Story about Ping* (3-6).

Fox, Mem, *Wilfrid Gordon McDonald Partridge* (4-7). A caring little boy helps an old woman find her lost memory.

Frost, Robert, *Birches*, ill. Ed Young (8-up), and *Stopping by Woods on a Snowy Evening*, ill. Susan Jeffers (3-up). Beautifully-done picture books of these individual poems.

Gerstein, Mordicai, *The Mountains of Tibet* (4-up). A boy grows up, dies, and chooses to return to the same valley in Tibet; inspired by the author's reading of the *Tibetan Book of the Dead*.

Gray, Nigel and Philippe Dupasquier, *A Country Far Away* (3-8). Parallel pictures bring out underlying similarities amid obvious differences in the daily lives of a European city boy and a rural African boy.

Greenfield, Eloise, *Grandpa's Face* (3-9). When she sees her actor Grandpa rehearse a very mean face, Tamika is afraid that someday he will look at her that way; a reassuring book.

Grifalconi, Ann, *Kinda Blue* (4-8). A little girl is lonely until her uncle explains that everything is individual and needs special attention.

Heide, Florence Parry and Judith Heide Gilliland, *The Day of Ahmed's Secret* (4-10). A boy who works all day waits till evening to tell his family a happy secret; pictures bring Cairo's streets alive.

—— *Sami and the Time of the Troubles* (4-10). Daily life of a boy and his family in war-torn Beirut shows the determination of people living in tragic chaos; beautifully illustrated.

Hendershot, Judith, *In Coal Country* (5-up). Reminiscences about growing up in a coal-mining town.

Henterly, Jamichael, *Good King Wenceslas* (all ages). Sumptuous illustrations enhance the familiar Christmas carol.

Herriot, James, *Moses the Kitten* (4-10). Love of animals comes through clearly in this story of an abandoned kitten adopted on a North England farm.

Hewett, Joan, *Rosalie* (4-8). Depicts a family's love for their very old dog.

Hickman, Martha Whitmore, *When Andy's Father Went to Prison* (5-9). The story of one boy addresses the concerns of children whose fathers are in prison, and gives understanding of children in that situation.

Hoose, Hannah and Phil, *Hey, Little Ant* (4-8). An ant tries to convince a boy to spare him; emphasizes compassion and empathy for all beings.

Jenkins, Emily, *Five Creatures* (3-8). Comparisons among members of a happy household of three humans and two cats.

Johnson, Angela, *When I Am Old with You* (3-8). A child thinks of all the things he likes to do with his grandfather.

Joslin, Sesyle, *What Do You Say, Dear?* (4-7). Delightful, absurd situations illustrate good manners.

Joyce, William, *Bently and Egg* (4-9). The adventures of a sophisticated frog looking after an egg for his friend, the duck.

Keats, Ezra Jack, *The Snowy Day* (2-6). A little boy explores his city neighborhood on a snowy day.

Kesselman, Wendy, *Emma* (6-11). A 72-year old woman takes up painting and finds great pleasure in it.

Kraus, Robert, *Herman the Helper* (3-7). A little octopus helps everyone around him.

—— *Leo the Late Bloomer* (6-10). Despite his father's worries, Leo learns to read, write, draw, and speak all in his own good time.

Krauss, Ruth, *The Big World and the Little House* (4-7). A family makes an abandoned house into a home.

Lasker, Joe, *He's My Brother* (5-11). Home and school experiences of a younger brother with a learning disability.

Leaf, Munro, *The Story of Ferdinand* (3-7). A gentle bull refuses to fight in the bull ring.

Lenzen, Hans Georg, *The Blue Marble* (5-10). A quiet boy is given a marble that stimulates his imagination and he then gives it to another child.

Lesser, Carolyn, *The Goodnight Circle* (4-8). Peaceful goodnight book recounting the cycle of the day-animals going to sleep and the night-creatures' activities.

Lindgren, Astrid, *The Tomten* (3-7). A Swedish tomte (gnome) visits animals and people on a farm one winter night. Also *The Tomten and the Fox*.

Picture Books

Lionni, Leo, *Frederick* (3-6). A poet-mouse stores up his own gifts for the winter.

—— *Little Blue and Little Yellow* (2-5). A story of friendship told with patches of color.

—— *Swimmy* (3-6). A different little fish finds a way to help the other fishes.

Lobel, Arnold. *Frog and Toad Are Friends* (3-7). One in a series featuring these friends and their adventures.

Loh, Morag, *Tucking Mommy In* (3-10). Reversing roles, two little girls help their tired mother get ready for bed.

Louchard, Antonin, *Little Star* (4-9). Wordless story of a starfish's adventures dreaming it is a celestial star, based on a poem by Hubert Michel.

Lyon, George Ella, *Who Came Down That Road?* (5-8). Mother and child ponder who might have traveled down an old, old road from pioneer days to prehistory in this beautifully illustrated book.

MacDonald, Golden, *The Little Island* (3-7). Although the island was little, it was part of the whole and had an important role to play.

Marshall, James, *George and Martha Encore* (3-7). One in a series of humorous, sensitive stories about two hippo friends.

Martin, Bill, Jr., and John Archambault, *Knots on a Counting Rope* (6-12). Close bond between a blind Navaho boy and his grandfather.

McBrier, Page, *Beatrice's Goat* (5-10). A family in Uganda receives a goat from Heifer Project International, which changes their lives; fact based.

McCarty, Peter, *Hondo & Fabian* (3-9). Hondo the dog goes to the beach to meet his friend, while Fabian the cat spends the day at home.

McCloskey, Robert, *Make Way for Duckling* (3-7), *One Morning in Maine* (4-7), and *Time of Wonder* (4-9). The inimitable ties between man and nature told with gentle charm.

McCourt, Lisa, *Chicken Soup for Little Souls: The Goodness Gorillas* (5-9). Classmates form a club to perform random acts of kindness, even for the meanest boy in class.

Minarik, Else, *Little Bear* (3-5). Warm relationships in a family of bears; one in a series.

Molk, Laurel, *When You Were Just a Heartbeat* (4-6). Anticipation for the coming baby in terms of the changing seasons; expectant parents may enjoy it also.

Mora, Pat, *Tomás and the Library Lady* (4-9). A child of migrant farm workers learns the wonder of books; based on experience of Tomás Rivera, a chancellor of the University of California.

Newberry, Clare Turlay, *Mittens* (3-7). When Richard finally gets a kitten, it becomes lost and finally found; beautifully illustrated.

Ormerod, Jan, *Messy Baby* (2-6). A sensitive father accepts the chaos produced by a very young child undoing his clean-up efforts.

——— *Moonlight* (2-7). Humorous, wordless book about parents putting a young child to bed. Also *Sunshine* (2-7).

Perkins, Lynne Rae, *Home Lovely* (5-8). Moving to an isolated mobile home, a little girl makes a garden with the help of the postman.

Pilkey, Dav, *The Paperboy* (4-10). A paperboy and his dog go through their early-morning routine together.

Piper, Watty, *The Little Engine That Could* (3-7). Success story about the little train that needed to get over the mountain.

Potter, Beatrix, *The Tale of Peter Rabbit* (3-7). First of the author's many beautifully written and illustrated stories; available in many editions. Favorites include *Mrs. Titlemouse, Jeremy Fisher*, and *Tom Kitten*.

Rayner, Mary, *Mr. and Mrs. Pig's Evening Out* (3-8). Mr. and Mrs. Pig leave their ten piglets with a new babysitter, Mrs. Wolf.

Richardson, Frederick, ill., *Mother Goose: Classic Volland Edition* (all ages). Beautiful, large, color illustrations make this Mother Goose extra-special.

Ringi, Kjell, *The Man Who Had No Dream* (4-8). A rich man is transformed by caring for an injured bird.

Rylant, Cynthia, *Appalachia: The Voices of Sleeping Birds* (6-up). Atmospheric paintings and text describe life in the mountains.

Say, Allen, *The Bicycle Man* (4-8). Two American soldiers in occupied Japan transform villagers' apprehension into friendship. Also *Grandfather's Journey* (4-12).

Sendak, Maurice, *Where the Wild Things Are* (3-7). How a little boy uses his imagination to handle the frustration of feeling helpless.

Seuss, Dr., *Horton Hears a Who* (3-7) and *Horton Hatches an Egg* (3-7). Stories about a conscientious elephant who believes "a person's a person no matter how small" and in keeping his word.

Picture Books

—— *How the Grinch Stole Christmas* (2-up). About the real meaning of Christmas.

Shaw, Charles G., *It Looked like Spilt Milk* (to 6). What are the white splotches on a blue background, which look like so many things?

Shulevitz, Uri, *The Treasure* (4-up). An old man discovers that "sometimes one must travel far to discover what is near." Also *Dawn* (3-up).

—— *The Magician* (5-10). Passover story of a poor elderly couple who entertain Elijah unawares.

Skorpen, Liesel Moak, *Mandy's Grandmother* (5-10). Mandy and her grandmother become good friends once each accepts the other for who she is.

Sonneborn, Ruth A., *Friday Night is Papa Night* (4-8). Warm story of a family looking forward to Papa's return from working all week at distant jobs.

Spier, Peter, *People* (4-8). Illustrations of people worldwide, with their many superficial differences, bring appreciation of our common humanity.

Spinelli, Eileen, *Somebody Loves You, Mr. Hatch* (7-12). Transformed by an anonymous valentine, a shy man finds his resulting helpfulness and friendliness make him many loving friends.

Steig, William, *Amos and Boris* (3-7). Friendship between a mouse and a whale in this variation of "The Lion and the Mouse." Also *Doctor de Soto* (4-10) and *Spinky Sulks* (4-10).

Steptoe, John, *Stevie* (5-8). Only after a younger foster brother has left does a boy realize his affection for him.

Stevenson, James, *Grandpa's Too-Good Garden* (4-8). When Louie and Mary Ann try to start a garden, Grandpa tells a tall tale about his first attempt at gardening with his younger brother. Also *Grandpa's Great City Tour* (3-7), an alphabet book.

Stolz, Mary, *Storm in the Night* (7-11). Warm relationship between a boy and his grandfather seen on a stormy night when the lights go out.

Thoreau, Henry David, *Walden* (5-10). Short selections from Thoreau's writings, accompanied by full-page linoleum-cut pictures, describe his life in the woods. Selections by Steve Lowe, ill. by Robert Sabuda.

Tolstoy, Leo, *Shoemaker Martin* (5-10). In this adaptation, a shoemaker wonders how he would welcome Jesus and learns that "as ye have done it unto the least of these my brethren, ye have done it unto me."

Tresselt, Alvin, *The Frog in the Well* (5-9). A frog finds there is much more to the world than living alone in his well.

—— *White Snow, Bright Snow* (3-6). Poetic treatment of events from the first snow through the coming of spring.

Udry, Janice May, *Let's Be Enemies* (4-7). Fed up with his friend's bossiness, John tells him they are enemies, but finds they are good friends indeed.

Ungerer, Tomi, *Crictor* (4-8). An old lady receives a boa constrictor from her son, which becomes a popular pet for the whole village.

Van Allsburg, Chris, *Just a Dream* (5-up). A thoughtless boy realizes the importance of caring for the environment after dreaming of a polluted future. Also *Polar Express* (all ages).

Van Leeuwen, Jean, *Amanda Pig and Her Big Brother Oliver* (3-7). A little sister who wants to do what her big brother does; one of a series.

Watson, Wendy, *Jamie's Story* (1-3). Wordless story of a little boy's day helping his parents.

Weigelt, Udo, *Bear's Last Journey* (3-8). A gentle treatment of a young child's reactions to a friend's last illness and death, told with animal characters.

Wells, Rosemary, *Shy Charles* (3-7). A happy, shy mouse refuses to speak to strangers, and his parents' efforts to make him sociable only make matters worse.

Wildsmith, Brian, *Hunter and his Dog* (4-8). A kind-hearted dog changes his master's outlook on hunting.

Williams, Vera B., *A Chair for My Mother* (4-8). A family saves to buy a special chair after a fire destroys all their furniture.

Wisniewski, David, *The Warrior and the Wise Man* (5-10). A Japanese emperor sets a quest for his twin sons, who are a contrast of brute force and reason; beautiful cut-paper illustrations.

Yashima, Taro, *Crow Boy* (5-10). Sensitive tale of rejection and acceptance.

Young, Miriam, *Miss Suzy's Easter Surprise* (3-6). A squirrel unexpectedly finds herself adopting four young squirrels.

Zolotow, Charlotte, *The Hating Book* (4-7). About friendship and misunderstanding.

—— *My Grandson Lew* (4-7). A boy and his mother realize grandfather's influence after his death.

—— *When the Wind Stops* (4-7). Cycles in nature and everyday life. Also *William's Doll* (4-7).

Fiction

(Including fictionalized autobiography; some
fiction also under Science and Nature)

Alcott, Louisa May, *Little Women* (10-up). Classic novel about family life and human relations.

Anderson, C. W., *Afraid to Ride* (8-12). After an accident Judy is too afraid to ride again, but recovers after a wise horseman gives her a horse to care for that has been ruined by over-training; beautifully illustrated.

Atwater, Richard and Florence, *Mr. Popper's Penguins* (6-10). Delightful story of the absurd consequences of a man's love for the Antarctic.

Austen, Jane, *Pride and Prejudice* (14-up). Witty novel about a man and woman overcoming misunderstanding, self-deception, and human foibles (their own and others'). Also *Emma* (14-up), *Sense and Sensibility* (14-up).

Avi, *Crispin: The Cross of Lead* (12-15). In this suspense novel set in medieval England, a 13-year-old boy flees false charges, finds an unexpected protector, and undergoes many adventures.

Bach, Richard, *Jonathan Livingston Seagull* (7-up). Symbolic story of aspiration and compassion.

Bailey, Carolyn Sherwin, *Miss Hickory* (6-up). Whimsical fantasy about a person with an apple-wood twig body and a hickory head, and her life with the animals of the New Hampshire countryside.

Barrett, William E., *The Lilies of the Field* (12-up). After stopping to help four German nuns working in a field, a young black man ends up building them a church.

Baudouy, Michel-Airne, *The Boy Who Belonged to No One* (12-up). An independent boy raised by construction workers learns that no one can be judged by appearances.

Baum, L. Frank, *The Wonderful Wizard of Oz* (5-up). First of the imaginative stories about Dorothy and the inhabitants of Oz. Also notable are *The Land of Oz*, *Ozma of Oz*, and *The Lost Princess of Oz*.

Becerra de Jenkins, Lyll, *The Honorable Prison* (12-15). A Latin American family held as political prisoners illustrates the vital importance of holding to individual values in attempting to overcome oppression, while not overlooking its cost; derived from the author's experience.

Bellamy, Edward, *Looking Backward* (15-up). Thought-provoking 19th-century Utopian novel with many interesting predictions and ideas about the future.

Benary-Isbert, Margot, *The Ark* (9-up). Happy story of a German refugee family that tries to find a place in their own country after WWII; a tribute to human will and spirit that overcomes misery and hardship. Continued in *Rowan Farm* (11-up).

—— *Castle on the Border* (12-up). In post-WWII Germany, a self-absorbed teenager learns to care for others while performing in a repertory company based at her aunt and uncle's country house.

Benchley, Nathaniel, *Bright Candles: A Novel of the Danish Resistance* (12-up). How the Danish people saved Jews in their country from the Nazis.

Bond, Michael, *A Bear Called Paddington* (4-8). Whimsical tales of a Peruvian bear living with a London family; first in a series.

Bosse, Malcolm J., *The Examination* (12-up). Adventures and trials of two brothers on their journey through 16th-century China to the capital so the elder can take the advanced government examination.

—— *Ordinary Magic* (12-up). A 14-year-old American, raised in India as a Hindu, comes to live in the Midwest after his father's death (formerly titled *Ganseh*).

Bothwell, Jean, *Little Flute Player* (8-12). How a Hindu boy saves his family in a time of famine.

Bridges, Sue Ellen, *Home Before Dark* (12-up). Teenage girl in a migrant worker family longs to hold on to her first permanent home; through her reactions to hardship, joy, sorrow, and new circumstances, she comes to realize the value of change.

Brink, Carol Ryrie, *Caddie Woodlawn* (9-up). Warm, adventurous tale of a tomboy growing up in a pioneer family.

Bronte, Charlotte, *Jane Eyre* (14-up). The life of an orphan, who overcomes a harsh childhood and discovers self-respect, independence, and love.

Buck, Pearl S., *The Big Wave* (9-14). After the destruction of his village, an orphan is cared for by his friend's family and comes to accept life again.

Fiction

Bunting, Eve, *The Empty Window* (8-12). By doing something for his dying friend, a boy conquers fear and uncertainty.

Burnett, Frances Hodgson, *Little Lord Fauntleroy* (6-12). A New York boy finds himself heir to an English earl and wins his grandfather's love.

—— *A Little Princess* (8-12). A wealthy girl reduced to poverty wins out through goodness and strong character.

—— *The Secret Garden* (6-12). Well-loved story of an unpleasant orphan and her hypochondriac cousin transformed by the magic of love, positive thinking, and wholesome activity.

Butler, Beverly, *Light a Single Candle* (13-up). Experiences of a 14-year-old girl on becoming blind: loneliness, sadness, and disbelief offset by courage and determination; the author is blind.

Byars, Betsy, *The Pinballs* (8-12). Three very different children change their attitudes with understanding foster parents, offering a promising future for all of them in this witty, happy book.

—— *The Summer of the Swans* (12-up). The problems of growing up, centering on a teenager's love for her retarded brother.

Cameron, Ann, *The Secret Life of Amanda K. Woods* (7-12). Girls will identify with this individualistic fifth-grader on the road to self-discovery in a flawed family.

Carlson, Natalie Savage, *The Family Under the Bridge* (8-up). A Parisian hobo befriends a homeless family at Christmas and grows to care about them in spite of himself. Also the Christmas story *Surprise in the Mountains* (4-10).

Caudill, Rebecca, *The Happy Little Family* (4-7). Five adventures of a four-year-old girl living in a log cabin with her sisters and brother.

Choi, Sook Nyul, *Year of Impossible Goodbyes* (12-up). Harrowing, exciting story of a family in occupied Korea which survives the Japanese occupation and flees to the South after WWII; based on the author's experiences. First of a series.

Clark, Ann Nolan, *Secret of the Andes* (9-up). A modern Inca llama herder learns about himself and his heritage on a journey to Cusco. Also *To Stand Against the Wind* (12-up).

Cleary, Beverly, *Henry Huggins* and *Ramona* series (7-12). Well-observed, humorous incidents in the lives of children, their friends and families; excellent family reading.

Clifton, Mark, *Eight Keys to Eden* (12-up). Top scientist, sent to investigate inexplicable happenings on an Eden-like planet, finds an unexpected key to consciousness.

Coatsworth, Elizabeth, *The Cat Who Went to Heaven* (7-up). A Japanese painter, a cat, and a miracle in a Buddhist setting.

Cole, Brock, *Celine* (12-up). Amusing story of a high-school junior to whom things seem to happen out of the blue, one after another. How she meets and solves all these events will cause readers to smile and root all the way for this heroine.

Collodi, C., *The Adventures of Pinocchio* (7-10). Classic about a live puppet's struggle to become a real boy.

Cooper, Susan, *The Dark Is Rising* series (10-up). This excellent fantasy series, blending realism and Celtic mythological themes, includes *Over Sea, Under Stone; The Dark Is Rising; Greenwitch; The Grey King;* and *Silver on the Tree*.

Coutant, Helen, *First Snow* (6-up). A Vietnamese girl learns the meaning of death and change.

Craik, Dinah Maria Mulock, *The Little Lame Prince* (5-11). A boy overcomes injustice and hardship to become a wise king.

Crane, Stephen, *The Red Badge of Courage* (14-up). Portrait of one young soldier's fear and bravery during a Civil War battle.

Craven, Margaret, *I Heard the Owl Call My Name* (12-up). A young clergyman's last years spent among the Indians of the Pacific Coast yield rich lessons.

Cronin, A. J., *The Stars Look Down* (15-up). A family of English miners experience poverty, ill-health, and needless accidents; finally the owners are forced to pay higher wages and follow safety rules.

Degens, T., *Transport 7-41-R* (12-up). A 13-year-old undergoes a risky journey from East to West Germany after WWII, and the decency, trust, and kindness of an old man give her new expectations.

De Jong, Meindert, *The House of Sixty Fathers* (10-up). A Chinese boy's bravery and ingenuity during his journey through enemy territory to find his family.

Dickens, Charles, *A Christmas Carol* (8-up). Miserly, selfish Scrooge is transformed by the ghosts of Christmas. Also *David Copperfield* (14-up).

Fiction

Dickinson, Peter, *Tulku* (12-up). During the Boxer Rebellion the son of an American missionary in China flees to Tibet with an eccentric English botanist and her Chinese servant, meeting with unusual adventures.

Druon, Maurice, *Tistou of the Green Thumbs* (4-up). Whimsical fantasy about a little boy who solves society's problems with his "green thumbs."

Dumas, Alexandre, *The Count of Monte Cristo* (14-up). Rousing tale of betrayal and vengeance, where the wronged hero in the end becomes self-regenerated, but only after destroying his false accusers. Also *The Three Musketeers* (12-up).

Ende, Michael, *The Neverending Story* (10-15). Fantasy-adventure about a boy who seeks to save Fantastica, then returns to his ordinary world with the ability to love.

Enright, Elizabeth, *Thimble Summer* (7-12). A Minnesota farm girl's experiences with her family and friends one summer in the 1930s.

Estes, Eleanor, *The Hundred Dresses* (8-12). Powerful treatment of intolerance, dignity, and compassion.

—— *The Moffats* (7-12). Warm, humorous episodes concerning a family which finds enjoyment although times are hard during WWI; first of a series. Also in the same setting, *Gynger Pye* and *Pinkie Pye* (7-12).

—— *The Witch Family* (6-11). Charming Halloween story interweaving the lives of two little girls and of Old Witch on the glass mountain.

Fife, Dale, *North of Danger* (10-15). A boy undertakes a 200-mile ski trip to warn his father of the German invasion of Norway in WWII; exciting tale of courage, survival, and trust, based on a true story.

Fine, Anne, *The Chicken Gave It to Me* (6-10). Humorous fantasy about a chicken who alerts two children and a planet of aliens to the inhumane treatment of farm animals.

Fisher, Dorothy Canfield, *Day of Glory* (14-up). Thought-provoking story emphasizing how we survive and triumph over adversity, through courage and self-forgetfulness.

—— *Understood Betsy* (7-12). An overprotected girl finds confidence, self-reliance, love, and understanding living with her cousins in Vermont.

Fisher, Robert, *The Knight in Rusty Armor* (12-up). Lighthearted allegory of a desperate knight trapped in his rusty armor, which takes the reader through the ups and downs of the struggle to understand life's meaning and come to self-realization.

Flory, Jane, *One Hundred and Eight Bells* (10-13). Portrait of an artistic girl in a traditional Japanese family; rich with descriptions of Asian beauty, customs, and values.

Forbes, Kathryn, *Mama's Bank Account* (12-up). Anecdotes about a Norwegian immigrant family full of warmth and self-forgetfulness.

Gannett, Ruth, *My Father's Dragon* (5-9). Elmer Elevator goes to rescue a baby dragon held captive by the animals on Wild Island; continued in *Elmer and the Dragon* and *The Dragons of Blueland*.

Gardiner, John Reynolds, *Stone Fox* (6-10). When his grandfather falls ill, a young boy tries to keep up the farm and enters the annual dog race to pay the back taxes; unexpected tragedy brings tears as well as thankfulness; easy reader.

Garfield, Leon, *The December Rose* (14-up). A young chimney sweep in Victorian London falls into a situation filled with murder, infamy, and espionage, and in the course of solving the mystery matures as a human being.

Gates, Doris, *Blue Willow* (9-up). Realistic story of a migrant worker family in the Depression, and the daughter's longing for a permanent home.

Godden, Rumer, *The Mousewife* (7-12). A house mouse befriends and frees a dove who widens her horizons.

Grahame, Kenneth, *The Wind in the Willows* (7-up). Timeless tale of friendship among the riverbank animals; beautifully written.

Grant, Joan, *Winged Pharoah* (13-up). Life of a royal woman of ancient Egypt, with many mystical aspects. Also *Life as Carola* (14-up).

Griese, Arnold A., *The Wind Is Not a River* (12-up). Sister and brother survive by themselves on the Aleutian Islands after the Japanese invasion, helping a wounded enemy soldier before escaping.

Harnden, Ruth, *The High Pasture* (12-up). City boy staying on his aunt's high-country ranch gradually accepts his beloved mother's death, and comes to appreciate his father.

Hartling, Peter, *Crutches* (12-15). Exciting tale of a 12-year-old Austrian boy separated from his mother after WWII and his relationship with a one-legged soldier; they support each other through hunger and real danger on the long journey to find the boy's mother; based on the author's life.

Haugaard, Erik Christian, *The Little Fishes* (12-up). Story of three Italian waifs during WWII reveals courage and the endurance of the human spirit. Also, the historical novel *Hakon of Rogen's Saga* (8-12).

Fiction

Hautzig, Esther, *The Endless Steppe* (12-up). Based on the author's experience as a Jewish girl deported from Poland to Siberia during WW II, reflecting the optimism and resilience of the human spirit.

Hemingway, Ernest, *The Old Man and the Sea* (13-up). Classic written from the heart, depicts strength, endurance, and the questioning of conviction toward one's life's work.

Herriot, James, *James Herriot's Treasury for Children* (4-12). A collection of Herriot's animal-story picture books in one volume.

Hodges, Margaret, *The Wave* (5-12). An old man burns his rice fields to warn villagers of a tidal wave; based on a tale of Lafcadio Hearn.

Holling, Holling Clancy, *Paddle-to the-Sea* (8-12). A carved wooden Indian and canoe travel through the Great Lakes to the Atlantic.

Hughes, Monica, *The Keeper of the Isis Light* (11-15). A human girl lives joyously on a far planet with her Guardian until settlers from earth arrive; thought-provoking examination of prejudice, acceptance, and rejection.

Hughs, Ted, *The Iron Giant: A Story in Five Nights* (5-9). A mechanical giant, pacified by a group of farmers, saves earth from a huge star-monster; notable drawings.

Hunt, Irene, *Up a Road Slowly* (11-14). A girl growing up learns that a life without kindness and love has little meaning.

Jarrell, Randall, *The Animal Family* (6-up). Exceptional story of a hunter and a mermaid, who live with a bear, a lynx, and a little boy. Also *The Bat Poet* (8-up).

Juster, Norton, *The Phantom Tollbooth* (8-up). A bored boy is swept into adventure in a fantasy kingdom; imaginative wordplay.

Kaplan, Bess, *The Empty Chair* (10-13). A 10-year-old Jewish girl loses her mother, then adjusts to her step-mother, sharing her thoughts, feelings, and schemes with readers in a sprightly way.

Kipling, Rudyard, *The Jungle Book* (5-up). Adventures of a boy raised by wolves in the Indian jungle, along with other animal tales such as "Rikki-Tikki-Tavi."

—— *Just So Stories* (4-up). Well-written, witty tales; many also available as individual picture books.

—— *Kim* (11-up). Anglo-Irish orphan's adventures in India with a Lama and the Secret Service.

Konigsburg, E. L., *Journey to an 800 Number* (12-up). A bright, snobbish boy is transformed by spending a month with his father, a camel-keeper.

Korner, Wolfgang, *The Green Frontier* (12-up). Fictionalized autobiography of an East German teenager whose parents crossed into West Berlin nine years before the Wall was built, telling of the confusion, resentment, and adaptability of youthful political refugees.

Krumgold, Joseph, *Onion John* (11-up). A small-town boy's friendship with a wise eccentric reveals to him and others that in trying to help another one must allow for individual freedom.

Lagerlof, Selma, *The Wonderful Adventures of Nils* (9-14). A cruel and lazy boy learns compassion and love of animals traveling around Sweden with a flock of geese while enchanted as a tomte.

Lampman, Evelyn Sibley, *The City under the Back Steps* (7-12). Two children become tiny and are forced to take an active role in the life of a colony of ants, whom they come to respect.

Lawson, Robert, *Rabbit Hill* (6-12). Warm, humorous fantasy about the small animals living around a country house, and the owners' kindness.

Lee, Harper, *To Kill a Mockingbird* (12-up). Coming of age story set against racial injustice in the South.

L'Engle, Madeleine, *A Wrinkle in Time* (9-14). Thought-provoking science fiction about remarkable children fighting the evil holding their father captive on a far planet. Continued in *A Wind in the Door* (9-14).

Lewis, C. S., *The Lion, the Witch and the Wardrobe* (7-up). Four children enter a frozen world and participate in a battle between good and evil in this Christian allegory; first of the *Chronicles of Narnia* series.

——— *Out of the Silent Planet* (13-up). Allegorical science fiction concerning an Englishman's fight against evil on Venus, and its strange races of inhabitants. Continued in *Perelandra* and *That Hideous Strength*.

Lewis, Elizabeth Foreman, *Young Fu of the Upper Yangtze* (10-14). A widow and her son move to the city, where he has adventures, dreams, and accomplishments; a beautiful description of old China.

Lifton, Betty Jean, *The Dwarf Pine Tree* (6-12). Set in Japan, this story tells of a tree's self-sacrifice.

Lowry, Lois, *Anastasia Krupnik* (9-12). Humorous events, at home and in school, in the life of a precocious and individualistic 10-year-old; first in a series.

Fiction

—— *The Giver* (12-up). In a painfree "utopia" a boy must receive mankind's memories from their elderly keeper; brings out the dehumanizing effect of seeking to abolish all pain, conflict, unhappiness, and personal choice.

—— *Number the Stars* (10-14). Suspenseful story of a Danish family hiding a Jewish girl during WWII.

Lyon, George Ella, *Borrowed Children* (12-15). Tender story of a poor, discontented 12-year-old in 1930s Kentucky who must care for her family after her mother nearly dies in childbirth.

MacDonald, Betty, *Mrs. Piggle-Wiggle* (5-12). A humorous look at children's behavior problems which are solved by a somewhat magical old woman; first of a series. Also *Nancy and Plum* (7-11).

Macdonald, George, *At the Back of the North Wind* (9-12). Young Diamond learns much in his nightly adventures with the North Wind.

—— *The Lost Princess: A Double Story* (7-11). An unappealing princess is swept into strange adventures, and returns home transformed.

—— *The Princess and the Goblin* (7-10). A princess and a miner boy defeat the designs of wicked goblins in this mystical tale.

MacLachlan, Patricia, *Sarah, Plain and Tall* (8-12). Well-told story of a mail-order bride brings out self-sacrifice, self-esteem, and family.

—— *Through Grandpa's Eyes* (4-10). A boy's visit to his blind grandfather gives insight into how the blind perceive the world.

Mahy, Margaret, *The Catalogue of the Universe* (11-up). Unlikely friendship between a high school boy and girl in this fascinating book.

Magorian, Michelle, *Good Night, Mr. Tom* (10-up). Abused boy evacuated to the countryside blossoms under the care of an old man in this moving story.

Malot, Hector Henri, *Nobody's Girl* (10-up). An orphan in France keeps her identity secret until she wins her grandfather's love through goodness, courage, and intelligence.

Mathis, Sharon Bell, *The Hundred Penny Box* (8-up). The love between a young boy and his very old great-great-aunt.

McKinley, Robin, *The Hero and the Crown* (11-up). Riveting tale of a kingdom where dragons still live and of the heroine-princess who slays them.

Miles, Miska, *Annie and the Old One* (7-11). A Navaho girl learns to accept death as part of the cycle of life.

Millman, Dan, *Secret of the Peaceful Warrior* (6-10). An old man teaches a boy how to handle a bully through courage and love.

Milne, A. A., *Winnie-the-Pooh* (5-up). Classic tale of Christopher Robin and his escapades with Edward Bear, Eeyore, Piglet, and other forest friends.

Moe, Barbara, *Pickles and Prunes* (12-up). A sensitive and unusual examination of the effects of dying and of death itself.

Montgomery, L. M., *Anne of Green Gables* (8-12). The relationship of an imaginative Canadian orphan with the elderly brother and sister who adopt her; first of a series.

Mundy, Talbot, *Om: The Secret of Ahbor Valley* (12-up). Stirring adventure story with mystical overtones set in 1920s India, involving a mysterious lama, his chela, and a British operative determined to uncover their secret. Also *The Devil's Guard* (14-up).

Naidoo, Beverly, *Journey to Jo'burg* (7-12). Story of the problems of native South African family life, rural and urban, under apartheid.

Namoika, Lensey, *April and the Dragon Lady* (12-up). Chinese-American high school girl copes with her manipulative, old-fashioned grandmother.

Naylor, Phyllis Reynolds, *The Keeper* (12-up). As his father becomes increasingly violent and delusional, a boy and his mother become fearful and isolated, and despair of having him involuntarily committed until the situation is resolved. Suspenseful but not depressing, the book encourages readers to ask others for help when it is needed.

—— *To Walk the Sky Path* (10-up). A young Florida Indian is torn between the traditional culture of his family and the demands of a modern public school.

Nesbit, E. S., *The Railway Children* (7-12). Riches to rags to riches tale of three Edwardian children who help in clearing their father of a false charge. Also *The Enchanted Garden* (7-12).

Neville, Emily Cheney, *Berries Goodman* (11-up). Explores friendship, anti-Semitism, and city vs. suburb.

Newton, Suzanne, *I Will Call It Georgie's Blues* (12-up). A troubled minister learns from his children the effects of his hypocrisy; a story of hope and regeneration.

O'Dell, Scott, *Island of the Blue Dolphins* (10-14). Historical novel about the resourcefulness of an Indian girl left behind to survive alone on an island off Southern California.

Fiction

- Ogiwara, Noriko, *Dragon Sword and Wind Child* (10-15). Using motifs from Japanese mythology, a story of the battle between the forces of heaven and earth.
- Orgel, Doris, *The Devil in Vienna* (12-up). The close friendship of the daughter of a Nazi storm trooper and a Jew; based on the author's experiences.
- Orwell, George, *Animal Farm* (13-up). Fable, using farm animals, about totalitarianism and the corruption of idealism by power. Also *1984* (14-up).
- Park, Linda Sue, *Single Shard* (12-up). Young boy in 12th-century Korea makes a long, dangerous journey which unexpectedly changes his life, promising to make his dreams come true.
- Paterson, Katherine, *Of Nightingales That Weep* (12-up). Daughter of a Samurai learns the emptiness of appearances and the importance of integrity, set in turbulent 12th-century Japan.
- —— *The Great Gilly Hopkins* (10-14). A rough, witty girl who has been shifted from one foster home to the next, learns to love and to accept her responsibilities from the unconditional love of her last foster-parent.
- Pfeffer, Susan Beth, *What Do You Do When Your Mouth Won't Open?* (12-up). Trials of a young girl who eventually masters her great fear of public speaking.
- Potok, Chaim, *The Chosen* (14-up). Two brilliant young Jews, sons of a Hasidic rabbi and a Zionist, begin with hate and finally achieve enduring friendship despite conflicts between their fathers; illuminates Jewish history and tradition.
- Preussler, Otfried, *The Satanic Mill* (12-up). Beggar boy in 17th-century Germany, lured to an isolated mill, finds the miller a magician running a black arts school; points out the value of love and courage.
- Raskin, Ellen, *The Westing Game* (13-up). Unusual mystery in which the will of an unpopular rich man challenges people to find his murderer; full of puzzles.
- Reaver, Chap, *Bill* (12-up). Teenage girl lives with her alcoholic moonshiner father and her wonderful dog; one day a door of opportunity begins to open for them.
- Reiss, Johanna, *The Upstairs Room* (11-up). Story of two Jewish sisters hidden by a farm family in Holland, told by the younger, with fine characterizations and realistic reactions that come from life-experience. Her family's post-war experiences are told in *The Journey Back* (11-up).

Robertson, Keith, *In Search of a Sandhill Crane* (10-14). A teenager from the city matures while staying with his aunt in the country.

Robinson, Veronica, *David in Silence* (10-13). Perceptive story of a deaf boy, new in town, and the relationships he forms with hearing children.

Rodgers, Mary, *Freaky Friday* (10-up). A 13-year-old switches bodies with her mother for a day in this amusing story.

Rostkowski, Margaret I., *After the Dancing Days* (12-15). The friendship of a teenager with a badly-deformed WW I veteran erases the young man's bitterness, clarifies her conflicts between service, honesty, and loyalty, and awakens deeper understanding and compassion in the hearts of her extended family. Also, *Moon Dancer* (12-14).

Rushdie, Salman, *Haroon and the Sea of Stories* (11-up). Exuberant wordplay highlights this fantasy about a boy's journey to give his father back the ability to tell stories.

Ruskin, John, *The King of the Golden River* (6-12). Allegory of greed and cruelty vs. kindness and goodness, centering on three brothers.

Saint-Exupery, Antoine de, *The Little Prince* (10-up). Mystical tale of a small visitor from another planet.

Salinger, J. D., *Franny and Zooey* (14-up). Youngest children in an unusual family, now grown up, help each other come to some realization of the meaning of life.

Sandoz, Mari, *The Horse Catcher* (12-up). The young hero, hating killing but loving to catch horses, eventually earns a position of honor and respect; describes Indian life and at-oneness with the earth, its bounty, and living things.

Saroyan, William, *The Human Comedy* (13-up). Warm, sad, funny tale of a family in California's central valley during WW II, with a feeling for the unity of all people and of all life.

Saunders, Marshall, *Beautiful Joe* (6-up). Warm "autobiography" of a mistreated dog at last leading a dignified, contented life; emphasizing the importance of loving care, this classic based on an actual dog helped change public attitudes toward animals.

Schami, Rafik, *A Hand Full of Stars* (12-15). Four years from the diary of a Christian teen in Damascus seeking to be a journalist despite repression, giving insight into family life, religion, love, and political and social conditions.

Fiction

- Schlee, Ann, *The Vandal* (13-up). Surrealistic view of the future — controlled by computers, without memory from day to day, without violence or emotion — and the few who dare to break out; a tribute to the humanness of present mankind.

- Sebestyen, Ouida, *Words by Heart* (12-up). A universal story of the risks of rising above prejudice, fear, and tragedy to grasp and affirm life.

- Seredy, Kate, *The Good Master* (7-11). Adventures of a lively girl who goes to live in the Hungarian countryside with her uncle's family; continued in *The Singing Tree*.

- ——— *Philomena* (5-9). An orphan follows her intuition in order to find her aunt in the city.

- Sewell, Anna, *Black Beauty* (7-11). Classic animal story of the ups and downs in a horse's life, told from the horse's viewpoint.

- Shaw, George Bernard, *Pygmalion* (14-up). Witty play about a linguistic professor's molding of a Cockney flowergirl comments on class and human relations.

- Shelley, Mary W., *Frankenstein* (13-up). Thought-provoking classic about a scientist's overweening ambition and his refusal to accept and love his creation.

- Shriver, Maria, *What's Wrong with Timmy?* (4-10). Story may help parents discuss questions about children with developmental disabilities.

- Shute, Nevil, *Pied Piper* (13-up). A man fleeing the Nazi occupation of France finds himself helping a group of children reach England.

- Shyer, Marlene Fanta, *Welcome Home, Jellybean* (10-up). The ups and downs when a mentally retarded teenager returns to live with her parents and younger brother; surprisingly humorous.

- Sidney, Margaret, *Five Little Peppers and How They Grew* (6-10). Classic story about a poor but close family who unexpectedly find prosperity and happiness; first of a series.

- Singer, Isaac Bashevis, *The Power of Light* (5-12). Eight beautifully told stories, set in Europe and America, convey something of the miraculous quality of the Hanukkah festival.

- Skurzynski, Gloria, *Good-bye, Billy Radish* (11-15). Friendship between Irish-American and immigrant Ukrainian boys in a WWI steel mill town, telling of the happiness and hardships of those days before labor laws.

Snyder, Zilpha Keatley, *The Egypt Game* (10-12). A young girl's adventures and friendships show the need for people to reach out to each other.

Sommerfelt, Aimee, *The Road to Agra* (12-up). A poor boy takes his young sister on a long, dangerous walk through India to get an eye operation; full of atmosphere, excitement, and Eastern wisdom.

Sperry, Armstrong, *Call It Courage* (8-10). Polynesian boy sails alone to a distant island on a quest to conquer his fear of the sea.

Spinelli, Jerry, *Maniac Magee* (12-up). Amusing yet serious story of a runaway boy, the fastest runner in the world, who comes to the city and accepts help wherever he finds it, among blacks and whites, eventually helping to avert racial conflict.

Spyri, Johanna, *Heidi* (8-10). Swiss orphan transforms the life of her grandfather and others around her, and overcomes adversity to return to her mountain home.

Staples, Suzanne Fisher, *Shabandu, Daughter of the Wind* (11-up). Story of the independent 11-year-old daughter of a camel trader, written with great empathy for the desert dwellers of Pakistan; continued in *Haveli*.

Steig, William, *Dominic* (9-12). A joyous journey with a most unusual dog as hero, illustrated by the author and filled with humor, generosity, and adventure.

Steinbeck, John, *The Grapes of Wrath* (14-up). The plight of the homeless fleeing the Dust Bowl in the 1930s, stressing the humanity of the poor and displaced.

Stevenson, Robert Louis, *The Strange Case of Dr. Jeckyll and Mr. Hyde* (13-up). Dramatization of the duality of human nature.

Stevenson, William, *The Bushbabies* (10-up). A young girl travels on foot through East Africa with an African herdsman and her beloved bushbaby; exciting and historical.

Strete, Craig Kee, *When Grandfather Journeys into Winter* (8-12). The bond of love between a wise old Indian and his young grandson in a world where ancient traditions are hard to maintain.

Taylor, Mildred, *Roll of Thunder, Hear My Cry* (10-15). Intense story of a black farm family surviving in 1930s Mississippi; first of a series.

Taylor, Sydney, *All-of-a-Kind Family* (8-12). Five sisters in a poor but happy Jewish family in turn-of-the-century New York; first of a series.

Fiction

Terlouw, Jan, *How to Become King* (10-14). A 17-year-old boy undergoes seven tests to become king in this satirical fantasy.

Tolkien, J. R. R., *The Hobbit* (7-10). Written especially for children, this book introduces Middle Earth and its inhabitants with an adventure of dwarves, a dragon, and stolen treasure.

—— *The Lord of the Rings* (11-up). The stirring, mythic adventure of the inhabitants of Middle Earth battling to prevent the triumph of the forces of evil; includes *The Fellowship of the Ring*, *The Two Towers*, and *The Return of the King*.

Travers, P. L., *Mary Poppins* (6-10). A mysterious nanny transforms the lives of the Banks family; first of a series.

Trevino, Elizabeth Borton de, *I, Juan de Parejo* (11-up). Story centering on Velazquez' African slave, who wins his freedom, throws light on the Spanish painter.

Uchida, Yoshiko, *A Jar of Dreams* (12-up). Japanese-Americans during the Depression deal with prejudice; set against a warm family background.

—— *Journey Home* (8-12). Based on the author's experiences, a Japanese-American girl and her family return from internment camp to begin from scratch, meeting prejudice, hard times, and happiness. The story is begun with the family's internment in *Journey to Topaz* (8-12).

Warner, Gertrude Chandler, *The Boxcar Children* (6-10). The adventures of four orphans left almost penniless, whose daring and resourcefulness lead to a delightful ending; easy-reader, first of a series.

Watkins, Yoko Kawashima, *So Far from the Bamboo Grove* (11-up). Gripping story of the hardships involved in a Japanese family's escape from Korea and their struggles in Japan after WWII; based on the author's life. Continued in *My Brother, My Sister, and I* (11-up).

Weiman, Eiveen, *Which Way Courage* (12-up). An Amish teenager, who does not fit into the patterns family and community demand, finds strength and courage; introduction to Amish beliefs and way of life.

Wells, H. G., *The Island of Dr. Moreau* (13-up). Suspenseful science fiction brings out the horror of vivisection and of scientific research divorced from ethics. Also *The Time Machine* (13-up).

Whelen, Gloria, *Chu Ju's House* (13-up). Chinese girl runs away from home to save her little sister, and by sheer will power and hard work at last finds success and serenity.

—— *Homeless Bird* (13-up). Hindu girl becomes a teenage virgin widow, and overcomes many obstacles before finding contentment; offers a deep understanding of India.

White, E. B., *Charlotte's Web* (7-up). Friendship between a pig and a remarkable spider who saves his life.

Wier, Ester, *The Loner* (10-up). The evolution of an outcast orphan, who learns that people do need each other.

Wilder, Laura Ingalls, *The Little House in the Big Woods* (5-10). First of the autobiographical stories about a pioneer family; full of worthwhile human values. Later books in the series are written for progressively older children.

Wilder, Thornton, *The Bridge of San Luis Rey* (15-up). Examination of the lives of the several people killed when a bridge collapses, asking the question: why *these* people?

Williams [Bianco], Margery, *The Velveteen Rabbit* (4-8). Right before it must be destroyed, a beloved toy is saved by becoming real.

Williams, Vera B., *Scooter* (7-12). Particularly well-told story of a spunky girl who moves to New York City with her mother and makes new friends.

Wojciechowska, Maia, *A Single Light* (12-up). In this touching tale of renewal, a deaf and speechless girl in rural Spain, rejected by those around her, eventually leads others to change their lives by allowing them to see themselves for what they really are.

Wyss, Johann, *Swiss Family Robinson* (9-up). Through ingenuity, humor, and optimism, a shipwrecked family survive their adventures on a deserted tropical island.

Yep, Laurence, *Dragonwings* (11-up). A boy growing up in San Francisco's Chinatown in the early 1900s comes to understand his father's obsession with flight, while the father realizes the importance of human relationships.

Yumoto, Kazumi, *The Friends* (11-14). Curious about death, three schoolmates observe an old man, which unexpectedly changes the lives of all four for the better.

Myths and Tales

Adams, Edward B., ed., *Two Brothers and Their Magic Gourds* (5-8). Korean tale of forgiveness and good triumphing over selfishness.

Aesop, *The Fables of Aesop* (all ages). Classic fables in many editions.

Andersen, Hans Christian, *Fairy Tales* (4-up). Many editions, both collections and picture books.

Arabian Nights (5-up). Several good collections of these classic tales are available, as well as picture books of individual tales.

Bailey, John, Kenneth McLeish, and David Spearman, comp., *Gods and Men: Myths and Legends from the World's Religions* (10-up). Thirty brief tales on the themes of creation, good and evil, and heroes and prophets.

Baker, Betty, *At the Center of the World* (7-12). Papago and Pima myths of creation of the earth and its inhabitants.

Beach, Milo Cleveland, *The Adventures of Rama* (7-up). Brief retelling of the Ramayana with illustrations from a 16th-century Mughal manuscript.

Bryson, Bernarda, *Gilgamesh* (8-up). Fine retelling of the Babylonian epic.

Burton, W. F. P., *The Magic Drum* (6-up). Well-told selection of Central African tales.

Cole, Joanna, comp., *Best-Loved Folktales of the World* (all ages). Two hundred fairy and folk tales from all over the globe, indexed by category (age, reading aloud, plot themes, etc.) and arranged by region.

Colum, Padraic, *The Children of Odin: The Book of Northern Myths* (7-up), *The Children's Homer* (7-up), and *The Golden Fleece, and the Heroes Who Lived Before Achilles* (7-up). Excellent versions of these traditions, illustrated with beautiful pen and ink drawings.

D'Aulaire, Ingri & Edgar, *D'Aulaire's Book of Greek Myths* (5-12) and *D'Aulaire's Norse Gods and Giants* (5-12). Lavishly illustrated retellings of the Greek and Norse myths are a good introduction for younger children.

—— *East of the Sun and West of the Moon* (5-10). Twenty-one traditional Norwegian folktales, well and simply told with humor.

De Armond, Dale, *The Seal Oil Lamp* (5-up). Eskimo tale that brings out respect for nature and animals.

de Gerez, Toni, *Louhi, Witch of North Farm* (3-7). Picture book of this tale from the Finnish Kalevala.

Dharma Publishing, *Jataka Tales* series (3-up). Individual tales with full-page color illustrations celebrate the power of compassion and wisdom.

Edmonds, I. G., *Trickster Tales* (5-up). Stories from many countries featuring trickster figures.

Gaer, Joseph, *The Fables of India* (8-up). Large collection of well-told tales taken from *The Panchatantra, The Hitopadesa,* and *The Jatakas*.

—— *The Adventures of Rama* (11-up). Retelling of the *Ramayana*.

Gifford, Douglas, *Warriors, Gods and Spirits from Central and South American Mythology* (10-up). Selection of tales from Amerindian cultures, with color illustrations; Schocken World Mythology series.

Goble, Paul, *Buffalo Woman* (4-up). Plains Indian tale shows the transforming power of love and the kinship of humans and animals.

Green, Roger Lancelyn, *Tales of Ancient Egypt* (9-up). Good retelling of many Egyptian myths and tales; informative prologue.

Grimm, Jacob and Wilhelm, *Fairy Tales* (all ages). Many editions of collections and individual tales.

Harris, Geraldine, *Gods and Pharaohs from Egyptian Mythology* (8-up). Egyptian myths and tales of the pharaohs, with color illustrations; Schocken World Mythology series.

Hillerman, Tony, *The Boy Who Made Dragonfly* (8-up). Zuni myth about a drought which ruined the corn crop, and a heroic boy who helped to rescue his people.

Hodges, Elizabeth Jamison, *Serendipity Tales* (7-12). A happy adaptation of Oriental stories based on a 16th-century Venetian work.

Hodges, Margaret, *The Golden Deer* (5-9). Picture book of one of the Jataka tales, telling how Buddha as a stag caused a king to respect all life.

Hoffman, E. T. A., *Tales of Hoffman* (8-up). Best known for "Nutcracker and the King of Mice" on which Tchaikovsky based his ballet, and Offenbach's opera, "The Tales of Hoffman." Imaginative and haunting stories with beautiful imagery and insights on human nature.

Myths and Tales

Homer, *The Odyssey*, trans. Robert Fitzgerald (11-up). Blank verse translation for adults that is clear and colorful enough to excite the interest of children.

Humphries, Rolfe, trans., *The Aeneid of Virgil* (14-up). A verse translation that captures the color and tone of this Roman epic.

Hutchinson, Veronica, *Chimney Corner Stories* (3-7). Many familiar stories in a version particularly suited for reading aloud, including "The Pancake," "Cinderella," and "Billygoats Gruff"; author of several other collections.

Hutton, Warwick, *Noah and the Great Flood* (3-7). Effectively illustrated retelling of the Bible story.

Jaffrey, Madhur, *Seasons of Splendor* (8-up). Hindu tales associated with festivals of the year, introduced with reminiscences from the author's childhood in India.

James, Grace, *Green Willow and Other Japanese Fairy Tales* (5-up). Fine selection of 38 tales, with color plates.

Khan, Noor Inayat, *Twenty Jataka Tales* (4-up). An excellent selection of these symbolic adventures of nonviolence and compassion.

Lang, Andrew, *The Adventures of Odysseus* (8-up). Well-told prose version of Homer's *Iliad* and *Odyssey* as one story.

—— *The Blue Fairy Book* (4-up). 37 tales including favorites from the Arabian Nights, Perrault, and many others; one of the series of "Color" Fairy Books.

Lanier, Sidney, ed., *The Boy's King Arthur* (8-12). Traditional retelling of the Arthurian legend adapted from Mallory's *Morte d'Arthur*; some archaic language.

Lattimore, Deborah Nourse, *Why There Is No Arguing in Heaven* (6-10). Picture book retelling the Mayan creation story.

Lester, Julius, *The Tales of Uncle Remus* (5-12). Contemporary retelling of the Brer Rabbit stories that keeps the spirit of the original, well illustrated; first of three collections.

Lum, Peter, *The Stars in Our Heaven: Myths and Fables* (12-up). Stories from world mythologies, including Babylonian, Egyptian, Greek, Chinese, Indian, and Norse, concerning many constellations and stars.

Manitonquat (Medicine Story), *The Children of the Morning Light* (7-up). Well-told Wampanoag tales from Massachusetts, covering creation of earth, man, seasons, and wanderings of the tribe.

Manton, Jo, and Robert Gittings, *The Flying Horses: Tales from China* (9-up). Spans the earliest folktales to a 20th-century incident.

Martignacco, Carole, *The Everything Seed: A Story of Beginnings* (4-up). Striking yet simple retelling of how the primordial seed "unfolded to become everything in the Universe."

Martin, Fran, *Raven-Who-Sets-Things-Right* (8-up). Good retelling of 10 Northwest-coast Indian tales, beginning with the creation; informative introduction.

Mayer, Marianna, *Beauty and the Beast* (6-10). Well-told, beautifully illustrated version of this classic tale.

Mayer, Mercer, *East of the Sun and West of the Moon* (3-10). Picture book skillfully combines elements from "The Frog Prince" and "East o' the Sun, West o' the Moon"; exquisitely illustrated.

Mayo, Gretchen Will, *Star Tales* (4-10). North American Indian legends about the stars and constellations.

McDermott, Gerald, *Anansi the Spider* (3-8) and *The Magic Tree* (4-8). Two dramatically illustrated, effectively told African tales.

—— *Arrow to the Sun* (3-up). Striking illustrations bring to life this insightful telling of a Pueblo Indian initiation tale. Also *Raven: A Trickster Tale from the Pacific Northwest* (4-8).

—— *The Voyage of Osiris* (7-up). The trials and triumph of Osiris and Isis, with the author's distinctive illustrations.

Morris, Kenneth, *The Fates of the Princes of Dyfed* (12-up). Retelling of the Welsh Mabinogion; continued in the *Book of the Three Dragons*.

—— *The Chalchiuhite Dragon* (12-up). A mysterious green dragon-stone signals the return of the legendary god-king Quetzalcoatl.

Pavlat, Leo, *Jewish Folktales* (7-up). Handsome anthology of stories based on the history, religion, and customs of the Jewish people.

Perrault, Charles, *Fairy Tales* (all ages). Available in collections and as individual picture books.

Richardson, Frederick, *Great Children's Stories: Classic Volland Edition* (3-7). Traditional European tales, such as "The Little Red Hen," "The Old Woman and Her Pig," and "The Straw Ox"; notable illustrations.

San Souci, Robert D., *The Faithful Friend* (5-10). West Indian folktale of two friends, black and white, who save each other through their loyalty, bravery, and goodness.

―――― *The Legend of Scarface* (4-10). Blackfoot Indian tale of a hero, unattractive in appearance, who triumphs through kindness, courage, and determination; notable illustrations.

Schwab, Gustav, *Gods and Heroes: Myths and Epics of Ancient Greece* (10-up). Translation of German standard work; more complete than most collections, told with simplicity and restraint.

Schwaller de Lubicz, Isha, *Her Bak* (14-up). Story of a boy's spiritual coming of age; vol. 1, subtitled *The Living Face of Ancient Egypt*, gives real insight into the life and culture of Ancient Egypt, while vol. 2, subtitled *Egyptian Initiate*, illuminates the religion of the inner sanctuary.

Seeger, Elizabeth, *The Five Sons of King Pandu: The Story of the Mahabharata* (12-up) and *The Ramayana* (12-up). Excellent retellings of these great Hindu epics. Though lengthy, both are necessarily abridgments, but faithful in spirit and content.

Serraillier, Ian, *Beowulf the Warrior* (10-up). Fine verse version of the Anglo-Saxon epic.

Shah, Idries, *World Tales* (5-up). Shows "the extraordinary coincidence of stories in all times, in all places"; informative notes and color illustrations.

Singer, Isaac Bashevis, *Naftali the Storyteller and His Horse, Sus* (10-up). Well-written, amusing stories with a Jewish setting give the reader a wonderful sense of this religious tradition through a mixture of wit and wisdom.

Sleator, William, *The Angry Moon* (4-8). Tlingit Indian tale of bravery and magic.

Steptoe, John, *Mufaro's Beautiful Daughters: An African Tale* (7-12). Cinderella tale of two village daughters — one loving, the other selfish — who journey to the city seeking to marry the King; picture book.

―――― *The Story of Jumping Mouse* (6-up). Plains Indian tale of a mouse's sacrifice to reach the far-off land; beautifully illustrated.

Storm, Hyemeyohsts, *Seven Arrows* (13-up). The inner meaning of Plains Indian symbology seen against the horrific disruptions of native life and spirit caused by contact with Europeans; illustrated with historic photos and color shield paintings.

Sutcliff, Rosemary, *Black Ships Before Troy: The Story of The Iliad* and *The Wanderings of Odysseus: The Story of The Odyssey* (7-up). Superior retellings of Homer's epics, brought to life by Alan Lee's dramatic, beautiful illustrations on almost every page.

Timpanelli, Gioi, *Tales from the Roof of the World* (5-10). Four Tibetan folktales offer a balance of humor, drama, and magic.

Traven, B., *The Creation of the Sun and the Moon* (7-up). Well-told version of ancient Mexican creation stories.

Troughton, Joanna, *Sir Gawain and the Loathly Damsel* (3-8). Quest of King Arthur, and Sir Gawain's self-sacrifice and kindness; beautifully illustrated picture book.

Westwood, Jennifer, *Gilgamesh and Other Babylonian Tales* (12-up). Includes the stories of Marduk and Tiamat, the Flood, Adapa and the South Wind, and Inanna in the Underworld; informative introduction and notes.

Wilde, Oscar, *The Selfish Giant* (4-up). Fable depicting the power of love and unselfishness.

Wolkstein, Diane, *The Red Lion* (6-12). Ancient Persian tale about facing what is before us; beautifully illustrated in the Persian miniature style.

Young, Ed, *Lon Po Po* (5-9). A Red-Riding Hood story from China, with expressive illustrations. Also *Seven Blind Mice* (2-6).

Zeeman, Ludmila, *Gilgamesh the King* (5-12) Picture book retelling the first portion of the myth of Gilgamesh; concluded in two further picture books.

Religions of the World

Franklin Watts, publisher, *My Heritage* series (4-8). Simple introduction to various religions through the eyes of a child growing up in each faith; new titles added occasionally.
    Aggarwal, Manju, *I Am a Muslim* and *I Am a Sikh*
    Lawton, Clive, *I Am a Jew*
    Pettenuzzo, Brenda, *I Am a Pentacostal*
    Roussou, Maria, *I Am a Greek Orthodox*
    Samarasekara, Dhanapala, *I Am a Buddhist*

Silver Burdett, publisher, *World Religions* series (9-up). The basic beliefs, history, customs, celebrations, sects, and daily life in six world religions; illustrated with color photos and drawings.
    Bahree, Patricia, *The Hindu World*
    Bancroft, Anne, *The Buddhist World*
    Brown, Alan, *The Christian World*
    Charing, Douglas, *The Jewish World*
    Singh, Daljit & Angela Smith, *The Sikh World*
    Tames, Richard, *The Muslim World*

Bach, Marcus, *Had You Been Born in Another Faith* (12-up). Splendid introduction to nine world faiths, encouraging the reader to "move into the spiritual habitude of another's mind and heart" and find that "the spirit inherent in religions is found to be one spirit when we truly put ourselves in the other person's place."

Buscaglia, Leo, *Seven Stories of Christmas Love* (12-up). Stories from the author's life that illustrate the importance of love and caring.

De Paola, Tomie, *The Parables of Jesus* (3-12). Picture book featuring 17 New Testament parables.

Edmonds, I. G., *Hinduism* (11-up) and *Islam* (11-up). Thorough introductions to the beliefs and history of these religions; author of many thought-provoking nonfiction books for young people.

Fellows, Lawrence, *A Gentle War: The Story of The Salvation Army* (11-16). The history, goals, and work of this Christian group.

Fitch, Florence Mary, *Their Search for God* (12-up). Sympathetic coverage of Hinduism, Confucianism, Taoism, Shinto, and Buddhism.

Freedman, Russell, *Confucius: The Golden Rule* (7-up). Confucius' life and ideas explained simply, and his influence on more equable government and opportunity for all people.

Ganeri, Anita, *What Do We Know about Buddhism?* (7-12). Introduction to the basic history, beliefs, sects, customs, texts, and stories of Buddhism, with many illustrations. Series contains books by the same author on Christianity, Hinduism, Islam, Judaism, Sikhism, as well as several ancient and traditional cultures.

——— *Buddhist Festivals throughout the Year* (7-12). Basic history and beliefs of Buddhism, and the main festivals of its practitioners; many illustrations. Series contains books by the same author on Christian, Hindu, Jewish, Muslim, and Sikh festivals throughout the year.

——— *The Guru Granth Sahib and Sikhism* (7-12). Discussion of Sikhism and its holy book. Also by this author, *The Tipitaka and Buddhism*, *The Ramayana and Hinduism*, *The Qur'an and Islam*, *The Torah and Judaism,* and *The Bible and Christianity*.

Gibran, Kahlil, *The Prophet* (13-up). Poetically expressed spiritual philosophy of life.

Glubok, Shirley, *The Art of India* (6-12). Introduces Indian art simply, in relation to the Hindu, Jain, and Buddhist religions; author of many introductory art books.

Kurelek, William, *A Northern Nativity: Christmas Dreams of a Prairie Boy* (6-up). Author-artist depicts the Nativity in various Canadian settings during the Depression, asking "If it happened there, why not here? If it happened then, why not now?" Thought-provoking, filled with compassion, and universal in its spiritual message.

Landaw, Jonathan, *The Story of Buddha* (5-12). Simply told biography communicates the atmosphere of Buddha's teachings and work.

Meredith, Susan, *The Usborne Book of World Religions* (11-up). Comprehensive information about all the major world religions, as well as some less well-known faiths, can serve as a quick reference for children and adults; illustrated.

Moses, Jeffrey, *Oneness: Great Principles Shared by All Religions* (12-up). Brief quotations from many world religions show agreement on 14 basic principles, such as the Golden Rule and God is within.

Religions of the World

Rice, Edward, *The Five Great Religions* (12-up). Contemporary look at Hinduism, Buddhism, Judaism, Islam, and Christianity, stressing the mystical.

Rossel, Seymour, *Judaism* (10-up). Informative introduction to the history, beliefs, holidays, and branches of Judaism.

Seeger, Elizabeth, *Eastern Religions* (12-up). Thoughtful presentation of the history and philosophy of Hinduism, Buddhism, Confucianism, Taoism, and Shinto.

Serage, Nancy, *The Prince Who Gave up a Throne* (5-9). Introductory biography of the Buddha, concentrating on his youth.

Singh, Mala, *The Story of Guru Nanak* (5-11). Life of the founder of Sikhism, stressing brotherhood, kindness, and good deeds.

Snelling, John, *Buddhist Festivals* (8-14). Discussion of Buddhist festivals throughout the year.

Ward, Hiley H., *My Friends' Beliefs* (10-up). This "young reader's guide to world religions" covers Jewish, Buddhist, Hindu, and Muslim traditions, while over half the book examines various Christian denominations.

Yolen, Jane, *Simple Gifts: The Story of the Shakers* (12-up). The origins, history, practices, and beliefs of this Christian sect, sympathetically but objectively told.

Poetry

Adams, Adrienne, comp., *Poetry of Earth* (all ages). Selections from great poets about the earth and its creatures communicate a sympathy for life and its oneness.

Adoff, Arnold, *All the Colors of the Race* (10-up). Sensitive poems exploring the feelings of a child whose father is white and whose mother is black.

Aldan, Daisy, comp., *Poems from India* (12-up). Wide selection from Sanskrit hymns, religious texts, and court poetry; old Tamil poetry; and modern verse.

Atwood, Ann, *Haiku-vision: In Poetry and Photography* (9-up). Uses the camera as an aid in developing a sense of oneness with nature and of poetry as an experience of the spirit.

—— *My Own Rhythm: An Approach to Haiku* (9-up). Introducing three Japanese master-poets leads to a discussion of the inner dimension of poetry and of our vision of life; with poems and photographs by the author.

Bierhorst, John, ed., *In the Trail of the Wind* (12-up). Valuable anthology of many North and South American Indian poems, songs, prayers, and incantations; notes and glossary. Compiler of many other collections of Native American material.

Blake, William, *Songs of Innocence* (5-up). Illustrated with colorful woodcuts by Harold Jones.

Burgess, Gelett, *The Goops and How to Be Them* (4-7). Tongue-in-cheek verses on manners and consideration for others.

de Gerez, Toni, *2-Rabbit, 7-Wind: Poems from Ancient Mexico Retold from Nahuatl Texts* (12-up). This unusual collection includes a historical note by the compiler. Also *My Song Is a Piece of Jade* (10-up) which contains a selection of poems side by side in English and Spanish.

Dickinson, Emily, *I'm Nobody! Who Are You?* (4-up). Picture book of the author's poems, selected for children.

Dunning, Stephen, Edward Lueders, and Hugh Smith, comps., *Reflections on a Gift of Watermelon Pickle and other Modern Verse* (9-up). Unusual selection of modern poems for young people.

Fisher, Aileen, *Cricket in the Thicket* (3-up). Sensitive, almost microscopic observations of flora and fauna.

Fleischman, Paul, *Joyful Noise: Poems for Two Voices* (7-up). Poems about insects written as duets for people to read aloud together.

Frost, Helen, *Spinning through the Universe: A Novel in Poems from Room 214* (10-14). The author writes a series of poems from the teacher and children of a fifth-grade class which reveal their lives and feelings.

Frost, Robert, *You Come Too* (8-up). This selection for young people includes many favorites.

Fyleman, Rose, *A Fairy Went A-Marketing* (3-up). Picture book with the theme of having and letting go.

Greenfield, Eloise, *Night on Neighborhood Street* (4-10). Gentle poems about the life of people in an African-American part of a city.

Hopkins, Lee Bennett, comp., *A Song in Stone: City Poems* (7-up). Poems celebrating city life, illustrated with photographs.

Hughes, Langston, *The Dream Keeper and Other Poems* (9-up). Selections for children from this poet's work.

Janeczka, Paul B., *The Place My Words Are Looking For* (12-up). Modern poets share their poems, thoughts, inspirations, and memories about writing poetry.

Khayyam, Omar, *The Rubaiyat of Omar Khayyam,* trans. William Fitzgerald (12-up). Persian Sufi poetry on the impermanence of life; many editions.

Larrick, Nancy, *Piping Down the Valleys Wild* (all ages). Fine anthology of classic and modern poems.

Lewis, Richard, comp., *Miracles: Poems by Children of the English-speaking World* (all ages). A collection testifying to "the power and value of the poetic vision that is an integral part of childhood."

—— *The Moment of Wonder* (11-up). Chinese and Japanese poetry on nature, landscapes, seasons, and man, illustrated with paintings by Chinese and Japanese masters.

—— *Out of the Earth I Sing* (8-up). Poetry and song of primitive peoples of the world illustrated with photos of artifacts.

Longfellow, H. W., *Hiawatha's Childhood,* ill. Errol Le Cain (4-7). Selections from Hiawatha's childhood as a picture book; a still briefer selection is available in *Hiawatha*, ill. Susan Jeffers (4-7).

Poetry

Mizumura, Kazue, *Flower Moon Snow: A Book of Haiku* (7-up). Haiku poems in praise of nature, illustrated with the author's woodcuts.

Moore, Lilian, *I Thought I Heard the City* (7-up). Poems expressing city moods.

Nye, Naomi Shihab, *This Same Sky* (14-up). Collection of poems about the natural world and its human and animal inhabitants, written by 20th-century poets outside the United States.

Opie, Iona and Peter, *A Family Book of Nursery Rhymes* (2-6). A treasury of 358 memorable rhymes illustrated on almost every page.

Plotz, Helen, comp., *Imagination's Other Place: Poems of Science and Mathematics* (12-up). Wonderful, often suggestive, selections on this unusual theme.

Poetry for Young People Series, Sterling Publishing Co. (11-up). Biography and selection of about 20 poems or parts of poems from each poet, with color illustrations; titles include *Henry Wadsworth Longfellow, Carl Sandburg, William Carlos Williams, Walt Whitman,* and *William Wordsworth,* among others.

Richardson, Frederick, ill., *Mother Goose: Classic Volland Edition* (2-up). Beautiful color illustrations make this Mother Goose extra-special.

Roberts, Elizabeth Madox, *Under the Tree* (4-11). Direct, timeless poems of childhood.

Stevenson, Robert Louis, *A Child's Garden of Verses* (all ages). This classic of children's poetry comes in many editions and abridgments.

Untermeyer, Louis, comp., *Rainbow in the Sky* (all ages). Large anthology of many favorite children's poems, with informative notes.

Volavkova, Hana, ed., *I Never Saw Another Butterfly . . .* (12-up). Children's drawings and poems from Terezi'n Concentration Camp (1942–44) portray the resilience of the human spirit while bringing home the tragedy of the death camps.

Watson, Clyde, *Father Fox's Pennyrhymes* (3-8). Simple, nonsense nursery-rhymes and detailed illustrations evoke the seasons in rural Vermont with whimsy and humor.

Whitman, Walt, *Voyages,* comp. Lee Bennett Hopkins (12-up). Over 50 selections span the poet's life and include some of his most famous verses; handsomely produced.

Wyndham, Robert, *Chinese Mother Goose Rhymes* (1-6). Charming translation of over 40 Chinese children's rhymes, riddles, and chanting games; fine illustrations.

Science and Nature

Nonfiction

Adamson, Joy, *Born Free* (12-up). The Adamsons raise a lion cub and prepare it for release to the wild.

Arnosky, Jim, *Deer at the Brook* (2-6). Picture book of deer introduces nature watching to young children. Also *All Night Near the Water* (3-6).

—— *Drawing from Nature* (12-up). Artist shares not only valuable techniques for drawing but also his love for and keen observation of nature; continued in *Drawing Life in Motion* (12-up).

—— *Secrets of a Wildlife Watcher* (11-up). Tells how to find animals and get close enough to watch them by explaining how they live.

Bash, Barbara, *Ancient Ones: The World of the Old-Growth Douglas Fir* (5-12). Picture book captures the atmosphere of the old-growth forest in describing the life cycle of the firs and the web of life they support.

Baylor, Byrd, *The Desert Is Theirs* (4-up), and *The Other Way to Listen* (7-up). These books bring out the oneness of nature and man, and ways of getting in tune with nature and oneself.

Billington, Elizabeth T., *Understanding Ecology* (8-12). This basic presentation explains "how all living things affect each other and the world they live in."

Bird, Christopher, *The Secret Life of Plants* (14-up). Brings together fascinating research on consciousness in plant life.

Boeke, Kees, *Cosmic View: The Universe in 40 Jumps* (6-up). A journey in scale to the limits of space and into the atom, imaginatively yet accurately done; provides a cosmic perspective on mankind.

Boone, J. Allen, *Kinship with All Life* (10-up). Real-life experiences showing the oneness of all life and how animals communicate with each other and with people who understand them. Also *Adventures in Kinship with All Life* (10-up).

Brown, Vinson, *Reading the Woods* (12-up). Encourages a sense of wonder through understanding the woods, explaining the influence of climate and weather, and how man and animals fashion woods. Also *Knowing the Outdoors in the Dark* (12-up).

Carrighar, Sally, *Moonlight at Midday* (15-up). Natualist visiting Northern Alaska for a year stays for ten because of her interest in and love for the people, native and settlers. Strong readers will find much of interest concerning the Alaskan people, land, and wildlife.

Darwin, Charles, *Voyage of the Beagle*, abridged by Millicent E. Selsam (12-up). Darwin's account of his formative journey around South America; edited for young people.

Duensing, Edward and A. B. Millmoss, *Backyard and Beyond: A Guide for Discovering the Outdoors* (10-up). A fascinating book filled with useful information as well as deeper insights into the wonders of one's own backyard; good index and bibliography.

Durrell, Gerald, *My Family and Other Animals* (10-up). Often hilarious stories from the author's childhood in Corfu, focusing on the natural habitat and his eccentric family and friends; very well written.

—— *Three Tickets to Adventure* (10-up). One of the author's many books about expeditions to collect animals for zoos, full of humor and love of nature; others include *The New Noah*, *The Whispering Land*, *The Drunken Forest*, etc.

—— *A Practical Guide for the Amateur Naturalist* (10-up). Walking tours through 17 environments illustrate many activities for the naturalist; full of hands-on knowledge.

Earth Works Group, The, *50 Simple Things Kids Can Do to Save the Earth* (6-12). Clearly presents ways children can respect and care for their home planet.

Facklam, Margery, *Bees Dance and Whales Sing: The Mysteries of Animal Communication* (5-10). Discussion of the ways in which a wide variety of animals communicate leads to an appreciation of the marvels and oneness of life. Also *Partners for Life: The Mysteries of Animal Symbiosis* (5-12).

Farre, Rowena, *Seal Morning* (11-up). Memoir of the author's life from 10 to 17 with her aunt and many wild pets in an isolated, North Scotland cottage. Remarkable descriptions of this silent, remote wilderness highlight her unusual adventures — most humorous, a few sad.

Fiarotta, Phyllis and Noel, *Snips and Snails and Walnut Whales: Nature Crafts for Children* (4-up). Crafts using natural materials such as pods, leaves, rocks, and shells.

Science and Nature

Goudey, Alice E., *The Day We Saw the Sun Come Up* (5-8) and *Houses from the Sea* (5-8). Sensitive handling of nature themes of day and night and of sea shells.

Grillone, Lisa, and Joseph Germaro, *Small Worlds Close Up* (all ages). Scanning electron microscope photos of 31 familiar objects informs while stimulating the imagination.

Hatchett, Clint, *The Glow-in-the-Dark Night Sky Book* (all ages). Eight star maps divided by season, with stars that glow for easy use outdoors in the dark; also maps with the constellations as imagined by the ancients.

Herriot, James, *All Creatures Great and Small* (13-up). Memoirs of a vet in Northern England, full of humor and love of animals; first of a series.

Hirschi, Ron, *Who Lives in . . . the Forest?* (2-4). Lovely photos invite the very young to look at animals in the forest; one of a series.

Hirst, Robin and Sally, *My Place in Space* (4-8). A brother and sister pinpoint their location on earth and in the universe for a skeptical bus driver.

Hogner, Dorothy Childs, *Endangered Plants* (10-up). Describes endangered North American plants and how to help preserve and enjoy them.

Jaspersohn, William, *How the Forest Grew* (6-12). A clearing becomes a climax forest over a period of 200 years in this picture book.

Jeffers, Susan, *Brother Eagle, Sister Sky* (5-12). Using words attributed to Chief Seattle, this beautiful picture book describes respect and love for the earth and concern about its destruction.

Kohl, Judith, and Herbert, *The View from the Oak: The Private Worlds of Other Creatures* (10-up). Tells how creatures from spiders to whales sense space and time, and communicate; written with humor.

Krupp, E. C., *The Big Dipper and You* (5-up). Gives readers of any age a ready and easy reference for finding our place in the physical universe. Also *The Comet and You* (5-up).

Lorenz, Konrad Z., *King Solomon's Ring* (12-up). Informative and amusing anecdotes about animals by one of the founders of modern ethology.

Maxwell, Gavin, *The Otters' Tale* (8-14). Appealing, factual account of three adopted otters, abounding in photos; based on the author's *Ring of Bright Water*.

Miles, Betty, *Save the Earth! An Ecology Handbook for Kids* (7-11). Discusses land, air, and water pollution, with projects that illustrate ecological problems and possible solutions.

Milord, Susan, *The Kids' Nature Book: 365 Indoor/Outdoor Activities and Experiences* (all ages). Informative, thoughtful, and originally presented, it sharpens observation of nature; ideal for family participation, black and white illustrations on every page.

Poortvliet, Rien, *Dogs* (8-up). The author's illustrations — some done for accuracy, others for humorous effect — and anecdotes about his own well-loved dogs make this an unusually appealing tribute to dogs of many types.

Pringle, Laurence, *The Gentle Desert: Exploring an Ecosystem* (8-12). Study of North American deserts, their plants and animals, and human impact on them; author of many nature and environmental books.

Provensen, Alice and Martin, *Our Animal Friends at Maple Hill Farm* (3-7) and *The Year at Maple Hill Farm* (3-7). Character and idiosyncrasies of the animals on the authors' farm, and their experience of the passing seasons in these picture books.

Rotner, Shelley and Ken Kreisler, *Nature Spy* (4-7). Photographs encourage youngsters to take a close look at the world around them.

Selsarn, Millicent, *Backyard Insects* (2-5), and *All Kinds of Babies* (2-5). Two of the author's appealing science books for the very young.

Simon, Seymour, *Hidden Worlds: Pictures of the Invisible* (5-up). X-ray, scanning electron microscope, telescope, and stop action are among the techniques used to gain an unusual view of the world.

——— *Look to the Night Sky: An Introduction to Star Watching* (5-up). This practical text helps children grasp the awesome magnificence of our solar system and universe.

Suzuki, David, *Looking at Plants* (7-12). Introduction to plants, with projects to help children discover nature for themselves. Also *Looking at Insects* (7-12).

Tresselt, Alvin, *The Gift of the Tree* (4-10). The process of an oak dying and returning to the soil, aided by many animals and plants, is poetically told in this picture book; formerly titled *The Dead Tree*.

Weiss, Malcolm E., *Sky Watchers of Ages Past* (10-up). Thoughtful discussion of how and why ancient peoples tracked astronomical objects, using various Amerindian, Egyptian, and Ancient European examples.

Wick, Walter, *A Drop of Water*, (6-up). Exceptional photographs and thoughtful text explain many characteristics of water, ice, snow, clouds, soap bubbles, etc., in this picture book.

Science and Nature

Fiction

Baker, Jeannie, *Window* (4-10). Wordless picture book of elaborate collages shows how a little boy's wilderness home in Australia is engulfed by the city as the years go by. Also *Home*.

Banks, Kate, *A Gift from the Sea* (5-11). With few words, this picture book suggests the many adventures a rock has undergone from the time of the dinosaurs till a boy finds it at the beach.

Blake, Robert J., *The Perfect Spot* (4-up). In this picture book, a boy and his artist father walk through the woods looking for the perfect spot to paint.

Burnford, Sheila, *The Incredible Journey* (9-up). The friendship among two dogs and a cat, and their will to survive, on a 250-mile trek through the Canadian wilderness.

Burningham, John, *Hey! Get Off Our Train* (3-9). Picture book where one night a boy and his dog go around the world on his toy train, letting endangered animals join them one by one.

Carrighar, Sally, *One Day on Beetle Rock* (12-up). Fictionalized but scientifically accurate account of a June day in the life of various members of the animal community in the High Sierras.

Cherry, Lynne, *The Great Kapok Tree* (5-11). Centered on the interdependence of rainforest life and the importance of preserving the trees.

Fish, Helen Dean, *When the Root Children Wake Up* (4-8). Beautifully illustrated story from the early 1900s about the waking of life in spring, its flourishing in summer, and its return to the earth in autumn.

George, Jean Craighead, *Julie of the Wolves* (11-14). An Eskimo girl, protected by wolves while lost on the tundra, gains appreciation of her heritage and her oneness with nature.

—— *My Side of the Mountain* (10-up). A city boy survives in the wilderness, learning about the plants and animals.

—— *Who Really Killed Cock Robin?* (9-14). An ecological detective story, where young investigators discover how interrelated seemingly separate or trivial environmental factors are.

Goffstein, M. B., *Natural History* (3-6). Simple, effective presentation of the brotherhood of all life.

Holling, Holling Clancy, *Pagoo* (6-9). The life story of a hermit crab, beautifully illustrated.

McNulty, Faith, *The Lady and the Spider* (4-8). A gardener spares a spider living in her lettuce plant; brings out the value of all life.

Morey, Walt, *Canyon Winter* (11-up). A city boy, stranded in the wild for six months with an old prospector, gains strength, understanding, and a true friend; plea for environmental responsibility and appreciation of nature.

Mowat, Farley, *Owls in the Family* (9-12). Humorous story of a boy's love of nature — especially animals — while growing up in Canada.

Robertson, Keith, *In Search of a Sandhill Crane* (10-14). A teenager from the city matures while staying with his aunt in the country.

Rounds, Glen, *The Blind Colt* (5-11). Tells how a blind wild colt survives his first year in the Badlands of Montana, finally to be befriended by a young boy; fine nature descriptions.

Salten, Felix, *Bambi: A Life in the Woods* (6-10). Classic story of a deer, and of man's impact on the forest.

Seton, Ernest Thompson, *Lives of the Hunted* (10-up) and *Wild Animals I Have Known* (10-up). Beautifully told, but often sad, stories of animals by a master nature author.

Seuss, Dr., *The Lorax* (4-8). Fable on the importance of preserving the environment.

Simon, Mina and Howard, *If You Were an Eel, How Would You Feel?* (3-6). Imaginative, poetic presentation of various animals.

Skofield, James, *All Wet! All Wet!* (3-7). Wordless story about nature seen by a small boy on a rainy day.

Smith, E. Boyd, *The Farm Book* (4-9). Simple story of two city children spending time on a farm, as well as beautiful, accurate illustrations, reveal New England rural life and values in 1910.

Tejima, Keizaburo, *The Bears' Autumn* (2-7). Striking double-page color woodcuts depicting a bear and cub fishing for salmon at night. Also *Owl Lake* (3-8).

Titchenell, Elsa-Brita, *Once Round the Sun* (5-9). Combining science with fun, Peter's "Big Year" provides many lessons about natural rhythms and phenomena.

Nonfiction and Biography
(Other nonfiction under Science and Nature; fictionalized biographies under Fiction.)

Alexander, Sally Hobart, *Mom Can't See Me* (5-up). From the point of view of her 9-year old daughter, the author tells her own story of living fully despite blindness; illustrated with photographs.

Aliki, *Mummies Made in Egypt* (5-12). Discusses ancient Egyptian beliefs on death, explaining how mummies and tombs were prepared.

Al-Windawi, Thura, *Thura's Diary: My Life in Wartime Iraq* (12-up). Memoir by a 19-year-old Iraqi girl of the 2003 US invasion of Iraq and its effects on the life of her family and friends.

Ancona, George, *Helping Out* (3-7). Photographs of children who are enjoying helping adults with many different types of work.

Atwood, Ann, and Erica Anderson, *For All That Lives* (7-up). Photographs illustrate brief quotations from Albert Schweitzer on reverence for, and the oneness of, all life.

Bartholomew, Carol, *My Heart Has 17 Rooms* (13-up). Autobiography of an American woman who helped at a small Indian hospital in the late 1950s.

Beard, Daniel Carter, *The American Boys Handy Book* (7-15). Reprint of 1890 manual covering making kites, aquariums, knots, boats, puppets, camping, fishing, etc., by the founder of Boys Scouts of America. Also *How to Amuse Yourself and Others: The American Girls Handy Book* by Adelia and Lina Beard (7-14).

Ching, Lucy, *One of the Lucky Ones* (11-up). Inspiring story of the determined struggle and triumph of a Chinese girl over blindness, superstition, and prejudice.

Churchill, Winston, *Heroes of History* (12-up). Sketches of notable historical figures compiled from Churchill's *History of the English-Speaking Peoples*.

Dolan, Edward F., Jr., *Animal Rights* (11-15). Discusses the moral issues concerning mankind's uses of and relations with animals.

Edmunds, I. G., *Second-sight: People Who Read the Future* (11-up). Intelligent discussion of prophecy in the West, covering Nostradamus, Jean Dixon, and Edgar Cayce in some depth.

Earnshaw, Ruth, and Katherine S. Kinderman, *In the Eye of the Typhoon* (15-up). Memoir of an American married to a Chinese professor living in China from the late 1930s through the Japanese occupation and Cultural Revolution, when her husband was blacklisted.

Epstein, Beryul and Samuel, *Who Says You Can't?* (12-up). Biographies of people in the 1960s who achieved public good through effort and vision.

Frank, Anne, *The Diary of a Young Girl* (11-up). Journal of a Jewish girl hiding from the Nazis in a secret Dutch apartment in WWII.

Freedman, Russell, *Kids at Work: Lewis Hine and the Crusade against Child Labor* (8-up). About one photographer's fight in the early 20th century to end child labor, including many of his evocative photos of the children themselves.

Gaes, Jason, *My Book for Kids with Cansur* (4-10). In this "Child's Autobiography of Hope," an 8 year-old shares his experiences with cancer in order to help other children; illustrated by his brothers.

Gandhi, M. K., *My Experiments With Truth* (14-up). Autobiography of the spiritual and personal struggles of India's great pacifist and patriot.

Gardner, Martin, *Aha! Gotcha: Paradoxes to Puzzle and Delight* (10-up). Paradoxes from logic, probability, numbers, geometry, time, and statistics intrigue and challenge reasoning power and intuition. Also *Aha! Insight* (10-up).

Gilbreth, Frank, Jr., *Cheaper by the Dozen* (10-up). Efficiency experts raise 12 children in this amusing reminiscence. Continued in *With Bells on Their Toes* (11-up) and *Time out for Happiness* (12-up).

Gold, Phyllis, *Please Don't Say Hello* (8-12). A family moving to a new neighborhood serves as a vehicle for this intelligent explanation of autism; by the mother of an autistic child.

Greenberg, Jan and Sandra Jordan, *The Painter's Eye: Learning to Look at Contemporary American Art* (12-up). Analysis by the authors and quotations from artists help readers gain an appreciation for the elements and principles of painting in contemporary art. Also *The Sculptor's Eye* (12-up).

Griffin, John Howard, *Black Like Me* (14-up). A white man, having medically darkened his skin, travels through the 1950s South as a black man.

Nonfiction and Biography

——— *A Time to Be Human* (12-15). A thoughtful examination of racism written for young people.

Heide, Florence Parry, and Judith Heide Gilliland, *The House of Wisdom* (5-9). Picture book about the famous library in 9th-century Baghdad, focusing on the boy who became the greatest translator of Aristotle's works into Arabic.

Hendrickson, Karen, *Baby and I Can Play* (3-12). Picture book acquaints older siblings with enjoyable activities they can initiate with an infant brother or sister, including positive things they can do when they resent the baby.

Henry, Madeleine, *Little Madeleine* (13-up). Interesting recollections of a girl growing up with her seamstress mother in 1920s France; first of a series.

Heyerdahl, Thor, *Kon-Tiki* (10-up). True adventure of sailing across the Pacific in a replica of an Incan raft to prove the ancients could have done so; available in youth and adult versions.

Hocken, Sheila, *Emma and I* (12-up). A young Englishwoman tells of her life as a blind person, and the difference her beloved seeing-eye dog made.

Hoose, Philip, *It's Our World, Too! Stories of Young People Who Are Making a Difference* (9-up). Profiles of many young activists who have acted on what they believe.

Keller, Helen, *The Story of My Life* (13-up). Autobiography shows forth the spirit of right living and thinking even under the worst adversities, and the wonderful relationship between Helen and her teacher.

Kennedy, John F., *Profiles in Courage* (11-up). Americans who stood for principle and acted on their convictions, whatever the consequences.

Kettelkamp, Larry, *Dreams* (10-14). Gives ancient and modern ideas on dreams, their significance, and their role in human life; author of many interesting nonfiction books for young readers.

Kherdian, David, *The Road from Home* (12-up). A son tells of his mother's experiences as the only member of her family to survive the Armenian massacres of WWI.

Koehn, Ilse, *Mischling, Second Degree: My Childhood in Nazi Germany* (13-up). Memoir of a Nazi youth separated from her father and his family because he was half Jewish; an inside look at growing up in Nazi Germany and a powerful indictment of war.

Konigsburg, E. L., *A Proud Taste for Scarlet and Miniver* (11-15). Unusual and effective biography of Eleanor of Aquitaine.

Krementz, Jill, *How It Feels When a Parent Dies* (7-up). Several young people share their experiences concerning the loss of a parent in the hope that it may help others feel less alone and unique.

Langone, John, *Death is a Noun* (14-up). Even-handed, journalistic discussion of death and related topics such as euthanasia, abortion, murder, suicide, and immortality; author of several good nonfiction books for young people.

Lansing, Alfred, *The Endurance* (12-up). Account of the disastrous voyage of Antarctic explorer Ernest Shackleton, and the incredible way in which no men were lost despite losing their ship and living for long periods on ice flows; a tribute to the human spirit.

Lapierre, Dominique, *City of Joy* (15-up). Powerful, moving account of the inhabitants of a Calcutta slum, revealing the tragedy and heroism of their everyday life.

Lester, Jules, *To Be a Slave* (12-up). Stories of US slavery, most told in the words of former slaves. This powerful indictment gives insight into African-American history and the horrors of slavery of any kind.

Maruld, Toshi, *Hiroshima no Pika* (9-up). A family's experience when the atomic bomb dropped on Hiroshima is movingly told in this picture book in the interest of peace. A powerful book, perhaps for younger children best read with parents.

McNeer, May, and Lynd Ward, *Armed with Courage* (8-12). Biographies of Florence Nightingale, M. K. Gandhi, George Washington Carver, Father Damien, Jane Addams, Wilfred Greenfell, and Albert Schweitzer.

Mebane, Mary E., *Mary: An Autobiography* (15-up). Through its details, this slow-moving autobiography allows readers to relive the experiences of an African-American girl growing up in rural North Carolina in the 1930s and '40s, who, with the encouragement of her aunt and father, overcomes horrendous obstacles to get a superior education.

Meigs, Cornelia, *Invincible Louisa* (10-14). Award-winning biography of Louisa May Alcott and her family.

Meyer, Edith Patterson, *In Search of Peace: The Winners of the Nobel Peace Prize 1901–1975* (12-up). Background on many individuals and organizations recognized for contributing to world peace.

Moody, Raymond A., *Life After Life* (15-up). Reports on people's near-death experiences and how common they are.

Peterson, Jeanne Whitehouse, *I Have a Sister — My Sister Is Deaf* (4-8). Explains simply what it's like to have a deaf sibling.

Nonfiction and Biography

Pirsig, Robert M., *The Zen of Motorcycle Maintenance* (15-up). Father's thoughts while on a cross-country trip with his son in search of truth and self-discovery.

Raynor, Dorka, *Grandparents around the World* (all ages). Full-page photos of grandparents and children from 25 countries.

Reuter, Margaret, *My Mother Is Blind* (5-10). A young boy describes how everyone in his family came to terms with his mother becoming blind; illustrated with photographs.

Richter, Elizabeth, *Losing Someone You Love: When a Brother or Sister Dies* (10-up). Sixteen young people who have lost a sibling share their feelings and difficulties in the hope of helping others in a similar situation.

Scholes, Katherine, *Peace Begins with You* (4-9). Simple presentation of what peace means and how we can each contribute to it.

Sís, Peter, *Starry Messenger: Galileo Galilei* (10-14). Picture book centering on Galileo's life, discoveries, and persecution by the Church.

—— *Tibet through the Red Box*, (10-up). Picture book centering on the author's father's diary of his adventures in Tibet right before the Chinese invaded.

Stowe, Leland, *Crusoe of Lonesome Lake* (13-up). A farmer and his family live isolated in the Canadian wilderness, building almost everything from scratch; fascinating, adventurous story of remarkable modern pioneers.

Thoreau, Henry David, *Walden*, selec. by Steve Lowe (5-10). Picture book with short selections from Thoreau's writings, accompanied by full-page linoleum-cut pictures, describe his life in the woods.

Weil, Lisl, *Wolferl: The First Six Years in the Life of Wolfgang Amadeus Mozart* (4-8). Picture book of Mozart's childhood at home and at the courts of Austria.

Wolf, Bernard, *Homeless* (4-10). Picture book of photos showing half a year in the life of an 8-year-old boy and his family in rent-free housing in New York City.

Yates, Elizabeth, *Amos Fortune, Free Man* (9-12). African slave in New England learns to read, eventually buys his freedom and later his wife's, and becomes a respected and successful tanner.

Resource Books for Adults

Allison, Christine, *Teach Your Children Well*. A well-rounded collection of excerpts from classic children's literature for reading aloud, organized around traditional values such as courage and kindness.

Armstrong, Thomas, *In Their Own Way*. Helps parents discover and encourage each child's learning styles, with many specific suggestions. Particularly good for parents of children labeled learning disabled.

Baldwin, Rahima, *You Are Your Child's First Teacher*. The author, a mother and former Waldorf teacher, gives both a practical and spiritual perspective on the issues of rearing preschool children.

Berends, Polly Berrien, *Whole Child/Whole Parent*. Applying the idea of the child as a spiritual being to daily problems of parenthood.

Bettelheim, Bruno, *The Uses of Enchantment*. Classic work on the importance of fairy tales to the psychological growth of the young child.

Bodenhamer, Gregory, *Back in Control: How to Get Your Children to Behave*. Presents practical, helpful strategies for avoiding manipulation and arguments, which allow parents to regain control of their children's misbehavior, even in very serious cases, in effective and appropriate ways.

Brookes, Mona, *Drawing with Children*. This "teaching and learning method that works for adults, too" enhances creative expression by showing how to analyze objects into five basic shapes.

Carson, Rachel, *The Sense of Wonder*. Words and photos help to keep alive the child's inborn sense of wonder and delight in nature.

Chukovsky, Kornei, *From Two to Five*. Scholarly yet simply-written observations of the intuitive literary processes and needs of the young child.

Cole, Robert, *The Spiritual Life of Children*. Author's talks with children reveal their innate spirituality and the ideas that many children have on religious subjects.

Copperman, Paul, *Taking Books to Heart: How to Develop a Love of Reading in Your Child*. A program to help parents encourage their children to want to read on their own and to succeed in reading at school. Also *The Literacy Hoax*.

Cornell, Joseph Bharat, *Sharing Nature with Children.* Imaginative activities to help children appreciate and empathize with nature.

Davis, Laura, and Janis Keyser, *Becoming the Parent You Want to Be: A Sourcebook of Strategies for the First Five Years.* Supportive and reassuring presentation helps parents assess their strengths and vulnerabilities, find their own vision of parenthood and family life, and work toward bringing it about.

Dyer, Wayne W., *What Do You Really Want for Your Children?* Practical strategies for raising "no-limit" children.

Edwards, Betty, *Drawing on the Right Side of the Brain.* Through practical exercises, the author effectively teaches older children and adults how to "see" — and therefore draw — like an artist, with emphasis on drawing people.

Elium, Don and Jeanne, *Raising a Daughter.* A spiritual perspective and a realistic psychological slant make this a good source for understanding how girls develop and what they need from their parents. Contains useful lists of further resources.

—— *Raising a Son.* Gives a practical yet inspirational and spiritually-oriented view on what it means to be a man, and how parents can help a boy achieve his positive potential.

Elkind, David, *The Hurried Child: Growing Up Too Fast, Too Soon.* Points out negative, stressful effects of pressuring children to cope, succeed, and understand, learn, or deal with situations and knowledge for which they are not yet ready.

—— *Miseducation: Preschoolers at Risk.* Examines dangers in pushing young children to learn school-age academic and physical skills; encourages age-appropriate activities that strengthen their spontaneous learning process and concept of self. Gives guidelines for evaluating preschool programs.

Eyre, Linda and Richard, *Teaching Children Sensitivity.* Designed to help preteens and teens "forget their own problems as they learn to help others." Also *Teaching Children Joy* and *Teaching Children Responsibility* apply to preschool and elementary school children respectively.

Friedman, Jenny, *The Busy Family's Guide to Volunteering.* Ways to involve the entire family in volunteer activities in many fields.

Fisher, Dorothy Canfield, *Mothers and Children.* Rich in commonsense philosophical values for those raising children today, although written 90 years ago.

Resource Books for Adults

Gray, John, *Men, Women and Relationships*. Illustrates and explains some basic differences between male and female approaches and psychology in order to improve understanding and allow more effective communication between men and women.

Hazard, Paul, *Books, Children, and Men*. A stimulating and rewarding volume for all interested in children and the books they choose.

Hickman, Danielle and Valerie Teurlay, *101 Great Ways to Keep Your Child Entertained While You Get Something Else Done*. Simple, fun ideas for independent play activities for indoors, outdoors, travel, and special occasions.

Jackson, Jane and Joseph, *Infant Culture*. A review of scientific studies on the consciousness and perception of very young children.

Kabat-Zinn, Myla and Jon, *Everyday Blessings: The Inner Work of Mindful Parenting*. Practical advice centering on awareness in the present moment and the unique potentials of each child.

Kohl, MaryAnn, *Scribble Art: Independent Creative Art Experiences for Children*. Gives instructions and ideas for over 200 open-ended art projects in all mediums. Also *First Art: Art Experiences for Toddlers and Twos*, for younger children.

Kubler-Ross, Elisabeth, *On Children and Death*. Offers insight and help in dealing with a child's death.

Lappe, Frances Moore, *What to Do After You Turn Off the TV*. Ideas for family activities for those who wish to decrease the time they and their children spend watching television.

LeShan, Edna, *When Your Child Drives You Crazy*. Practical advice for parents, drawn from the author's experience as well as her professional expertise.

Lewis, Hilda Present, ed., *Child Art*. A collection of essays on children's art as expressions of self-affirmation and inner development.

Lickona, Thomas, *Educating for Character*. Argues the importance of encouraging ethics and good character in the classroom, and the dangers of value-neutral education.

Lindbergh, Anne Morrow, *Gift from the Sea*. This little book, inspired by "the primeval rhythms of the seashore," helps many families find "creative pauses" in their complex lives.

Montessori, Maria, *The Discovery of the Child*. Montessori's books offer an inner perspective on educating the child helpful to parents and teachers.

Muller, Brunhild, *Painting with Children*. Instructions from an anthroposophic standpoint for introducing young children to colors and watercolors.

Nelsen, Jane, *Positive Discipline*. Adler-based philosophy advocating democratic decision making, natural consequences, and consistent follow-through by adults. Also, with H. Steven Glenn, *Raising Self-Reliant Children in a Self-Indulgent World*.

Orlick, Terry, *The Cooperative Sports and Games Book*. Over 150 games and ideas for adults as well as children providing "challenge without competition" by focusing on team goals and sharing.

Rockwell, Robert E., Elizabeth A. Sherwood, and Robert A. Williams, *Hug a Tree and Other Things to Do Outdoors with Young Children*. Helping young children learn about the natural world and how to care for it.

Sawyer, Ruth, *The Way of the Storyteller*. Invaluable to parents who want to help keep their children sensitive, perceptive human beings through the use of stories; includes several excellent tales to tell.

Sierra Madre Community Nursery School, *Nurturing Human Growth*. Many thoughtful ideas on enabling the development of the preschool child.

Steichen, Edward, comp., *The Family of Man*. Classic work of photography showing the oneness of mankind.

Tingley, Katherine, *Theosophy: The Path of the Mystic*. Contains sections on the home and the child from a spiritual perspective, simply and directly expressed. Also *The Gods Await*.

Toch, Thomas, *In the Name of Excellence: The Struggle to Reform the Nation's Schools*. Discussion of educational problems, why they persist, and possible solutions.

Verny, Thomas, with John Kelly, *The Secret Life of the Unborn Child*. Scientific findings showing the consciousness of the unborn child and the importance of the attitudes of parents toward, and their interactions with, the unborn and newborn child.

Warner, Sally, *Encouraging the Artist in Your Child (Even if You Can't Draw)*. Over 100 home projects for children 2 to 10 which help parents facilitate their children's creativity.

Some Sources for Finding More Children's Books

Besides browsing in the children's section at libraries and bookstores, and asking librarians, teachers, and friends for suggestions, many annotated lists of children's literature are available. Some are more selective than others and they address different needs. Anthologies and books about children's literature often contain good bibliographies also. While some of these books can be found in bookstores, most are available in libraries, on the shelves or at the librarian's desk. A few are:

Arbuthnot, May Hill, Margaret Mary Clark, Harriet G. Long, and Ruth M. Hadlow, *Children's Books Too Good to Miss*. An excellent selection of books for preschool through 14; annotated.

Association for Library Service to Children, *60 Years of Notable Children's Books*. Arranged by decades from the '40s to the '90s, with appendix of theme lists and author-title index.

Gillespie, John T. and Christine B. Gilbert, *Best Books for Children: Preschool through Middle Grades*. A large annotated list of both fiction and nonfiction books. John Gillespie has authored many bibliographies for children and young adults.

Lima, Carolyn W. and John A., *A to Zoo: Subject Access to Children's Picture Books*. Subject index of picture books.

Lipson, Eden Ross, *The New York Times Parent's Guide to the Best Books for Children*. Over 900 books with annotations, indexed by age as well as subject, author, illustrator, and title.

Miller-Lachmann, Lyn, *Our Family, Our Friends, Our World: An Annotated Guide to Significant Multicultural Books for Children and Teenagers*. About 1,000 fiction and nonfiction titles from 1970–1990, arranged by ethnic and national groups.

National Council of Teachers of English, *Adventuring with Books: A Booklist for Pre-K–Grade 6*. An extensive, useful annotated work organized by type and subject. Appearing about every four years, it gives the best books published since the last edition.

Silvey, Anita, ed., *Children's Books and Their Creators*. Excellent reference which concentrates on 20th-century children's literature, mainly alphabetical by author but with some subject headings.

Steiner, Stanley F., *Promoting a Global Community through Multicultural Children's Literature*. Annotated lists on cultures around the world, refugees, literacy, and books that bring people together, with suggested extensions for parents and teachers.

Trelease, Jim, *The New Read-Aloud Handbook*. Discusses reading aloud and lists a large selection of books especially recommended for that purpose.

Wilson, Elizabeth, *Books Children Love*. Worthwhile, well-written fiction and nonfiction books organized into 24 subject areas; helpful descriptions reveal the author's Christian background.